I0821167

Weird Catholic Handbook

Michael Lichens

Weird Catholic Handbook

SOPHIA INSTITUTE PRESS
Manchester, New Hampshire

Cover and interior design: Emma Helstrom

Sophia Institute Press
Box 5284, Manchester, NH 03108
1-800-888-9344
www.SophiaInstitute.com

Sophia Institute Press is a registered trademark of Sophia Institute.

Hardcover ISBN 979-8-88911-350-8

ebook ISBN 979-8-88911-351-5

Library of Congress Control Number: 2024946152

Fourth printing

Acknowledgments

HIS BOOK WOULD have been impossible to write without the encouragement and help of many good people. I hope I haven't forgotten anyone, but know that I am forever grateful if you gave me even a single word of encouragement.

First and foremost, I want to thank Charlie McKinney, Tom Allen, and the entire editing team at Sophia Institute Press for helping me to build up on the initial idea for this book and for taking a chance to let me write it. Of course, I'm also thankful for the hard-working editorial team who showed me patience and kindness as I wrote my first book.

I'm also grateful to Thomas L. McDonald, David Mills, and other Catholic writers who repeatedly encouraged me to write about these weird and overlooked topics. I'm especially grateful to Kevin Knight for running New Advent, which I used to find sources, and for telling me about the Wizard Clip haunting in a pub so many years ago.

I am blessed to have been educated by some incredible teachers, and I was thinking about all of them in the course of writing this book. I am thankful for all of them. Some educators, such as Stratford and Léonie Caldecott, also encouraged my work as a writer, and I don't think I could have written this without them. May God reward all the great teachers out there.

Finally, I am thankful for my parents and family, who supported me while I was writing this book and who helped me to cultivate the sense of wonder that led me to discover these stories and places. Aunt DeAnna and Grandma told me many wild and wonderful stories from Catholic history, some of which I talk about in this small book. I'm also grateful to my brother, Bob, and his wife, Becky, who both went above and beyond in encouraging me while I wrote this book. I owe a big round of thanks to David and Matthew, my other brothers, as well, for giving me a place to write and for celebrating my writing milestones with me.

Contents

PART 3

Spiritual Warfare and Catholic Campfire Stories

PART 4

Unusual Miracles

PART 5

A Weird Catholic Pilgrimage

Weird Catholic Handbook

Introduction

HIS BOOK IS the product of two great passions in my life, the first being my faith. The Catholic Faith has had a powerful impact on me, and I consider myself to be a devout Catholic, although I'm currently far from being a good one, as I often fail at living up to even the basic teachings, like charitability toward others.

The other great passion that inspired this book is my love of finding weird historical sites. When I say weird, I mean odd, unusual, or overlooked, and I nearly always use that term affectionately. For me, the weirdest parts of history often provide the best stories to retell. I seek out odd historical sites both in my own neighborhood and whenever I am traveling through Europe. This means that I've subjected friends and family to a lot of stopping on trips to see a historical marker of a forgotten battle or to take pictures of an old house that people say is haunted.

These two passions led to my tracking down stories and places from Catholic history that many would call weird, such as shrines in the Rockies that didn't even have Wikipedia pages, old crypts, tales of monsters, accounts of ghosts and demons, and all other sorts of overlooked stories from Catholic history. I shared a lot of these stories and places with people in person, on social media, and in articles over the years, and I was often surprised at how many people enjoyed hearing about these tales and historical sites.

I had the idea to write this book when I visited Italy. My Italian journey started in Milan, where I made a stop to see the Sanctuary of San Bernardino alle Ossa, a small chapel decorated with bones, also called an ossuary. I had been to several other ossuaries before, but this was the first time I had ever had one to myself. Seizing the opportunity to be alone, I sat and prayed for some moments, calmly and peacefully contemplating my life and the reality of my mortality before just sitting and taking in the beautiful chapel.

Eventually, a couple of polite tourists came in, snapped a few pictures, and left after a few minutes. Having heard how many tour guides leave out the spiritual significance of ossuaries and only describe them as macabre tourist attractions, I wondered what those tourists thought of this place. At that moment, it occurred to me that there should be a guidebook written about the spirituality of ossuaries and other strange Catholic sites.

I had only stopped in Milan that day on my way to make a pilgrimage to Assisi for the feast day of St. Francis, my patron. I attended a feast day Mass in the Basilica above St. Francis's tomb, and I visited the tombs of St. Clare and Bl. Carlo Acutis, who are both buried in the Umbrian hill town. I was praying for many things that day, for myself and for others, and I was overwhelmed by the beauty and history of Assisi and its many saints. However, I was also constantly thinking about my idea to write a guidebook.

On the train ride back to Rome, I realized I was on a sort of weird Catholic pilgrimage. While the main purpose of my trip was to see St. Francis on his feast day and to visit other saints and churches in Italy — in many ways, a typical pilgrimage for modern Catholics — I was also planning to see crypts, a museum for the souls in Purgatory, and other ossuaries in Italy. These are incredible places of

Catholic history, but they don't often get thought of as places to see on a pilgrimage. Yet these places had a powerful impact on me, and I couldn't think of why I shouldn't think of them as stops on my pilgrimage.

My initial idea for a travel guidebook soon grew and turned into a love letter to the strange yet sacred Catholic places I've seen and the weird stories I've enjoyed, stories that I think tell us a lot about the Catholic Faith and are in themselves a sort of weird pilgrimage through Catholic history and tradition. As you read, I hope that you become inspired to make a weird Catholic pilgrimage of your own.

While this book is written from a Catholic perspective, it is not dogmatic. If you are an orthodox Catholic, you don't have to believe in monsters or ghosts, no matter how many stories I share. You also don't have to go see a bone church, although I think you should, since they can be spiritually enriching. However, I hope you can get past any initial feeling of weirdness to see a beautiful part of our Faith and embrace whatever lessons you can learn from reading about this part of our history.

Likewise, if you are not Catholic, I hope you can appreciate these stories and places as weird and wonderful parts of Catholicism. From the outside, so much of Catholicism can be strange and even alien to non-Catholics, and these tales are no exception. However, learning about these weird places and tales will teach you a lot about the faith that has had an impact on countless cultures. You may not ever attend Mass or see a church except on vacation, but I hope this book tells you more about our dearest beliefs.

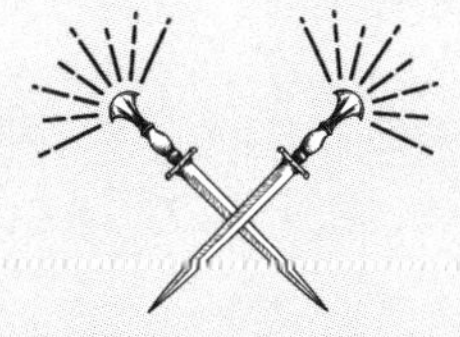

Part 1

Saints, Angels, and Monsters

"The baby has known the dragon intimately ever since he had an imagination. What the fairy tale provides for him is a St. George to kill the dragon."

— G. K. Chesterton, *Tremendous Trifles*[1]

SIDE FROM ST. George and the dragon, we often don't think of saints as monster fighters today. In our age of materialism and consumerism, saints are supposed to be quiet and demure figures who help us get more stuff. Saints help to answer prayers and decorate our churches. They certainly aren't supposed to go out with the cross and sword to do battle with the unknown.

But our early Christian forebearers would have found our modern ideas strange. The first saints were the martyrs, people like St. Peter the Apostle or St. Ignatius of Antioch who suffered horrific and public deaths while proclaiming the glory of Jesus Christ, and the cult of the martyr remained a powerful force for much of early Christianity. As modern literary critic Terry Eagleton summarizes, "The New Testament is a brutal destroyer of human illusions. If you follow Jesus and don't end up dead, it appears you have some explaining to do."[2]

One of those great martyrs was St. George himself. Long before he was depicted as a slayer of dragons, George of Lydda was a soldier in the Roman Empire who, in the fourth century, gave up a life of worldly honor for the truth of Christ. For his troubles, George was

1 G. K. Chesterton, *Tremendous Trifles* (London: Methuen and Co., 1909), 86.

2 Terry Eagleton, *Reason, Faith, and Revolution: Reflections on the God Debate* (New Haven, CT: Yale University Press, 2009), 27.

beheaded during the Diocletian persecutions, refusing to renounce his faith even in the face of death. George's witness led to many conversions in his own time.

Long after his martyrdom, St. George continues to inspire conversions, and he also inspires the converted to live a more radically authentic life in Christ. George was of course not the only Roman soldier who became a saint and died while preaching the love of God, but the legend of him overcoming the dragon made this Cappadocian Greek soldier the best-known among military saints, and his devotion endures to this day. By the time of the First Crusade, the soldier-saint had been adopted as a patron for armies across the world. The Republic of Genoa and the Kingdom of England would adopt his flag; places from Dragon's Hill, England, to Lydda, Syria, had landmarks proclaiming his works; and the legend of St. George and the Dragon became the source of stories, paintings, liturgical plays, and folk songs.

St. George died a martyr, for which he is justly celebrated, but we often only know of him because we've heard the tale of him slaying the dragon. We will dive deeper into the tales of St. George later in this book, but let's first consider why the legend of St. George the Dragonslayer is so enduring and influential.

The Power of Stories

Catholicism is a religion with a vibrant story-telling culture. This tradition goes back to the Gospels, wherein Our Lord taught profound lessons through His parables, and it continued with art, music, drama, and literature telling thousands of stories from the Bible, the lives of saints, and holy legends. These stories enrich our homes and our churches while they help us to understand the greatest story: when Love Himself rescued humanity from darkness.

The stories I'm about to share with you are not on the level of Christ's parables. However, they function similarly. They may not be factual, but they tell a more profound truth than just a list of facts. Much in the way that first-century people in Roman Judea didn't need to know the name of the Good Samaritan or the birthdate of the Prodigal Son, I don't need you to believe in dragons and werewolves. You simply need to hear the stories and truly consider them.

While all these stories are fantastic and give us a glimpse into the rich imagination of our ancestors, they have inspired the faithful to live better lives. As you read, try to hear each story as a Christian would in ages past. See St. George defeating the dragon as a parable for conquering sin (as many will hear in sermons) or as a lesson that evil — whether interior (such as sin or temptation) or exterior (violence and calamity) — exists but can be defeated. All of us will endure evil in some form. Most of us, Christian or not, are probably undergoing some kind of crisis right at this very moment. These stories from the Christian past not only accepted the reality of evil but gave us an escape, and they also called us to endure and overcome our present darkness.

These fantastical stories of saints overcoming monsters were a comfort to our ancestors, from the medieval peasant to the mendicant friar. Like us, they lived in a chaotic world that included drudgery, warfare, plague, and economic strife, yet they found relief in communal activities like storytelling. And so the stories of saints taking down monstrous creatures didn't just entertain them but gave them a parable for their own struggles and the strength to overcome them.

St. Michael the Archangel
defeats an ancient serpent.

Chapter 1

St. Michael: The Ideal Monster-Slayer

Now war arose in heaven, Michael and his angels fighting against the dragon; and the dragon and his angels fought, but they were defeated and there was no longer any place for them in heaven. And the great dragon was thrown down, that ancient serpent, who is called the Devil and Satan, the deceiver of the whole world — he was thrown down to the earth, and his angels were thrown down with him.

— Rev. 12:7–9

HIS FAMOUS PASSAGE from the Revelation of St. John depicts Satan as a dragon who was cast out of Heaven by St. Michael the Archangel. In just this short passage, you can already start to understand the archangel as an archetype for saintly monster fighting. The dragon, that deceiver of the world, also sometimes a representation of chaos and disorder, is defeated by the power of God, the creator of the universe who brings order and harmony with Him.

This biblical vision is literal and depicts an actual event. But as with so many biblical visions, St. John's is rich in symbolism and meaning beyond the literal narrative. We will see patterns from his vision in Christian stories of dragons and monsters, in which Satan himself is the archetype of the dragon or ancient serpent who spreads death, deception, and chaos. Only heroically spiritual people can defeat these monsters.

St. Michael's defeat of the dragon has been depicted in Christian art for millennia. While his appearance and depiction would change each century, almost always the archangel is portrayed as stabbing the dragon at his feet. Any Christian who has heard the story from the Bible can recognize St. Michael in art, but what many don't know is that St. Michael also has a habit of appearing to people in times of distress.

There is a cave on the slopes of Monte Gargano in Apulia, Italy, that has had a supernatural reputation since at least the time of the Romans. Pagans worshiped at the entrance of the cave long before Christianity came to the Italian peninsula, and it retained its mystical atmosphere even after the conversion of the people.

In the fifth century, as the Roman Empire was coming apart in the West, a nobleman came to St. Lorenzo Maiorano, the bishop of nearby Siponto, with news of an odd occurrence near this cave. Depending on which account you read, either the nobleman or his servant shot an arrow at a bull who refused to leave the entrance of the cave, only for the arrow to reverse, fly back to them, and injure the archer himself. Either way, the nobleman was troubled and sought the bishop's help. The saintly bishop knew that something was not right and immediately ordered the faithful to take on three days of prayer and penance.

At the end of the third day, the mighty St. Michael appeared to St. Lorenzo and commanded him, saying,

> Know ye that this man is so hurt by my will. I am Michael the archangel, which will that this place be worshipped on earth, and will have it surely kept. And

> therefore I have proved that I am keeper of this place
> by the demonstrance and showing of this thing.[3]

St. Lorenzo then made a procession to the entrance of the cave, where he offered prayers and praise. The bishop was still nervous about entering the cave, given its reputation, but St. Michael was not finished yet. Two years later, St. Michael appeared again to promise the people protection from a barbarian invasion. After several days of prayer and penance, a strong storm of hail fell on the invading army and caused them to leave St. Lorenzo and his people alone.

In gratitude, St. Lorenzo and the people made another prayerful procession to the entrance of the cave, where St. Michael appeared yet again. The archangel told the saint that the cave had now been consecrated to God, and he asked the bishop to build a church. When St. Lorenzo entered the cave for the first time, he found an altar and a cross and knew the archangel had kept his promise.

After receiving permission from the pope, St. Lorenzo built a church at the front of the cave and consecrated it to St. Michael. The shrine is still there on Monte Gargano, and there have been more apparitions of the archangel since the time of St. Lorenzo. Stones from the cave have even been considered relics and are used in exorcisms.

There are other famous shrines to St. Michael's apparitions in Europe, perhaps the most popular being Castel Sant'Angelo in Rome. What was once a mausoleum for Roman emperors and their families is now a popular tourist attraction near the Vatican. The Castel has a great statue of St. Michael at the top to commemorate an

[3] Adam Blai, *The Catholic Guide to Miracles* (Manchester, NH: Sophia Institute Press, 2021), 89. Mr. Blai got this account from *The Golden Legend*, a thirteenth-century hagiography.

apparition of the archangel to Pope St. Gregory the Great, which signaled the end of a plague.

While Castel Sant'Angelo and other European shrines are worth a visit, there is one holy site closer to home for us in the Americas. A couple of hours east of Mexico City, in the state of Tlaxcala, the town of San Miguel del Milagro hosts a shrine to St. Michael and his seventeenth-century apparition to a young convert named Diego Lázaro de San Francisco on April 25, 1631. Like the apparition to St. Gregory in Rome, this one was also related to an epidemic that had been decimating the people. St. Michael told the young man that he would provide a miraculous well in a ravine whose waters would cure disease, and he asked the young Diego to spread the word.

Diego was still a teenager and came from a native family, so the young man did not think that anyone would listen to him. He doubted himself and did not tell anyone about the mystical vision. Soon after the first apparition, however, Diego himself fell ill with a burning fever and was greatly weakened. A few days into his illness, on May 7, St. Michael appeared to him once again.

This time, many people saw the archangel in his glory. He was aloft in white light, and fear fell over Diego's family. The archangel took Diego by the hand and transported him to the site of the sacred spring, where a beam of light illuminated the spot in the ravine. Diego was given water from the spring that, through the grace of God, cured him of his terrible illness. St. Michael then took Diego back to his hut, and now he obeyed St. Michael and began to share news about this miracle.

Unfortunately, many people had trouble believing that the great St. Michael was appearing to this young man, and, once again, Diego Lázaro felt defeated. However, St. Michael was still not finished. In a final apparition, on November 13, the archangel spoke to Diego during Holy Mass and chastised him for not following his instructions.

So the young man went and collected some water from the miraculous spring and presented it to the bishop of Puebla. The bishop listened to Diego's story and took the spring water from him. The bishop then gave the water to several people suffering from disease, and they were miraculously cured. More investigations were carried out, and there were numerous stories of miraculous cures.

Soon, a shrine was built in what is now the town of San Miguel del Milagro. The people of the small town still hold processions in thanksgiving to St. Michael's intercession, especially on September 29, the Feast of the Holy Archangels.

As you can see, the mighty archangel is a popular patron saint, especially during times of plague or warfare. He is also a saint of spiritual warfare and is often invoked in exorcisms and blessings. Even when we do not face plague or warfare, we should still be able to turn to St. Michael in times of uncertainty and remember his holy example.

St. George and the Dragon
Cappadocia, Turkey

Chapter 2

The Saints Who Slew Dragons

AMONG THE ICONS found in Vinica, in north Macedonia, is a sixth-century terracotta relief depicting two saints, St. George and St. Christopher, slaying two dragons. Each saint stands holding a spear that pierces a serpent at his feet; St. George holds a round shield in his right hand, St. Christopher carries a cross in his left, and St. Christopher's head is portrayed as that of a dog (more on that in chapter 5). Both Christopher and George were early Church martyrs whose true deeds are known only to God, yet devotion to them was strong in the Eastern Roman Empire and gained great popularity in the West after the First Crusade, especially after many Crusaders reported seeing St. George ride with them at the Siege of Antioch in 1098. While we know very little about the actual lives of each of these martyrs, the Vinica icon shows that the legends concerning their dragon-slaying are ancient and that these heroic saints were incredibly influential in early Christianity.

The story of St. George and the Dragon probably originates after the saint's martyrdom. The legend goes that in Cappadocia (modern-day central Turkey), a fearsome dragon appeared and demanded tribute from the villagers. The villagers soon ran out of livestock and trinkets to leave for the dragon, so they started leaving live humans as a sacrificial tribute for the beast. One of the people to be sacrificed to the dragon was a princess.

St. George was riding through the region when he heard about the plight of the princess and the villagers. The Christian warrior had no fear of the ancient monster and promised to save the princess and rid the region of the dragon. With his armor and lance, St. George rode into battle as the dragon let out a fearsome cry. Yet with one well-placed stab of his lance, St. George slew the dragon, who fell under the hoofs of the saint's horse. The terrible beast was killed, and the princess was saved.

This legend spread throughout Christendom, and other locales would host their own tale of St. George and the Dragon. Beneath an ancient chalk horse in Uffington, England, for example, is a small hill called Dragon Hill, on whose summit St. George is said to have slain a dragon. No grass will grow here to this day because of the toxic blood spilled from the beast. Other places such as France and Libya also developed their own tales of St. George and his dragon-slaying prowess.

St. Christopher is the patron saint of travelers. While early iconography shows him also slaying a dragon, he is best known for being a giant from Canaan that unknowingly carried the Christ Child across a rushing river. His dragon-fighting might have been more symbolic, a way of representing to the faithful their own struggles against sin and evil and the victory guaranteed to those who hope in Christ and carry Him in their hearts. Whether as a giant or a dragon-slayer, St. Christopher, whose name means Christ-bearer, is a patron saint for many who want to also bear Christ on their journey.

There are also more slayers of dragons in the Communion of Saints. For instance, the *Acts of Philip,* a fourth-century apocryphal text, tells the story of St. Philip the Apostle confronting a dragon in Hierapolis, a holy city for Greek pagans in Asia Minor where a famed temple to Apollo had been constructed. According to the text, St. Philip came to this temple and cast out the demonic dragon that had been living there. The dragon was chased away, and many people began to believe in Christ.

St. Romanus of Rouen, France, a seventh-century bishop, scribe, and wonderworker, is also said to have defeated a dragon. St. Romanus had only the power of the Cross when he arrived in Rouen and found that the people were being terrorized by a river dragon called La Gargouille. The saintly bishop wanted to get rid of the beast and asked for volunteers to accompany him, but the people were so terrified that only one person volunteered, a condemned man. St. Romanus and the condemned man made their way to the river to confront the dragon. The dragon charged at them, but suddenly the saint made the sign of the cross. The dragon instantly stopped. St. Romanus held a crucifix while the two men bound the dragon and forced it back to town, where the people helped to kill and burn the dragon. However, the dragon's head was resistant to flame and stayed preserved. The city of Rouen then placed the dragon's head on the town walls. To this day, Rouen uses the monster as a town symbol, and for centuries, the people commemorated St. Romanus's helper by pardoning a convicted felon during Lent each year.

There are even more saints who are known to slay dragons, and they all follow familiar themes. Medieval Christians understood these stories as parables to explain the order of God chasing away the ancient chaos and darkness of the pagan past. The stories also symbolize the victory of Christ over the spirits of this world and bear spiritual implications for all the faithful. All these dragons share similarities with the original dragon of Revelation, the devil, and in these Christian tales, sometimes just the sign of the cross is as powerful as the sword of St. Michael to defeat dragons and chase away evil.

St. Nicholas and the miraculous revival and resurrection of the boys in the pickle barrels

Chapter 3

St. Nicholas, the Pickle Barrel, and a Devilish Tree

HEN YOU READ the name of St. Nicholas, you probably think of a jolly man in a red suit with a bag full of presents. While the saint is the origin of Santa Claus, the real St. Nicholas is so much more than Yuletide imagery. St. Nicholas of Myra was a fourth-century bishop, theologian, and ardent defender of orthodoxy. According to some legends, he was present at the Council of Nicaea, where he defended the doctrine of the Trinity and struck the heretic Arius. He was also known for his charity and miraculous works, so much so that the Eastern Church often refers to him as St. Nicholas the Wonderworker.

St. Nicholas was also an exorcist who subdued many monstrous spirits. When he became a bishop, he found that demons were haunting many old shrines in his city. Wherever he went, he knocked down idols and exorcized the buildings that had housed them. When people came to him with family members possessed by demons, St. Nicholas would make the sign of the cross over them, and the demons would leave. There are even multiple accounts of St. Nicholas exorcising haunted objects.

One story tells of St. Nicholas freeing people from a demon-haunted cypress tree in the village of Plakoma.[4] Some accounts say that this tree was an object of worship before Christianity, but either way, the villagers were now plagued by a powerful demon that inhabited the tree. St. Nicholas went to the tree, carrying the Gospels in his left hand. With his right hand, he made the sign of the cross; then he picked up an ax and cut down the possessed tree. The demon shrieked and quickly fled the town. People were so amazed that a nearby village asked the holy man to come deliver them from their demon-possessed tree as well.

One of the more horrific stories of St. Nicholas involves the deaths of three young boys. A monster of a man had murdered the boys, then butchered them and hid their remains in pickle barrels. The great St. Nicholas was having none of this, so he made the sign of the cross above the barrels. Miraculously, the boys were wholly restored and resurrected before an amazed crowd. This legend is also thought to be the inspiration for why you may find pickles and pickle barrels in modern Christmas decorations.

We find the true power of St. Nicholas over monsters, though, in some other Christmastime traditions. In places throughout central Europe, custom has it for St. Nicholas to visit on the eve of his feast day, during the season of Advent, to give gifts to good children and maybe quiz them on their Catechism. However, St. Nicholas doesn't come alone. Bound to the saint is a terrifying, horned monster.

There are many tales about this beast, and they differ a bit, depending on where you are. However, these monsters always have horns, hooves, and a tail. In German lands, he is called *Krampus,* while he is called *čert* in Czechia, but his name is often translated as

4 There is some debate about whether this story relates to St. Nicholas of Myra or St. Nicholas of Sion, who were often combined in hagiographies.

"devil" in English. The monster was fully subdued in other tales of St. Nicholas, and now it walks with him to chase, lash, or try to put naughty children in his large bag. This playful tradition has had a lot of recent attention on the internet, where the horror imagery is more emphasized. Still, St. Nicholas, thankfully, always has the devil under his control. So the good boys and girls never have to worry about the monster, but it might still scare the younger ones into behaving better.

There are many more miracles and spiritual fights that are attributed to St. Nicholas, and the tales didn't stop after his death. As we'll cover in a later chapter, the relics of St. Nicholas inspired more stories of his miraculous intercession. How many of these tales are true is a subject of ongoing debate, but the spirit of his work, his charity, and his fierce defense of the Faith shine through in every one.

St. Patrick driving snakes out of Ireland
Ireland

Chapter 4

St. Patrick: Apostle to the Irish and Demon Chaser

ST. PATRICK'S DAY is a massive cultural event in the United States and other nations. Chicago will dye their river green, and many more cities will host large parades. Of course, there is also revelry with green beer. Historically, all this was done in honor of the patron saint of Ireland, but most people forget that St. Patrick was a real person with a great impact on the early Christian Faith.

Most of what we factually know about St. Patrick comes from two of his writings, the *Confessio* and *Epistola*. There are, of course, other writings attributed to the saint, but there is great debate about the authorship of these. What we can tell from these writings is that Patrick was born in Roman Britain in the fifth century and was taken captive and sold into slavery in Ireland. After years of captivity, Patrick was able to escape and make it back to Britain, but he would soon have dreams of the Irish people asking him to come back and save them.

In Patrick's lifetime, Ireland was at the very edge of the known world. In the imagination of Christian Rome, it was a land of warring, petty kings, pirates, and slavers. And of course, it was also a land of old gods and monsters. We know now that the ancient people of Ireland were advanced in many ways, and they were influenced by continental Celts, Romans, and other civilizations. However, for St. Patrick, going back to Ireland meant trying to save the people of the land that held him captive. It was a great act of mercy that would reverberate for centuries.

The historical deeds of St. Patrick would be enough for his memory to remain eternal. He spread Christianity among the Irish, established several important monasteries, and set up the Irish monks to found monasteries across Continental Europe, from the North Sea to Vienna. Several of these monasteries still function today, representing centuries of unbroken tradition in which the monks not only spread the Faith but also preserved knowledge of Greek, manuscript illumination, and much more.

Still, we also know St. Patrick because of the numerous legends associated with him. The most famous might be the tale of St. Patrick driving snakes out of Ireland. As with most of these traditions, this story has questionable authenticity, but I think it still tells us a lot about St. Patrick from a spiritual warfare perspective, as it tells of St. Patrick's great power over the serpent, an ancient symbol of the diabolical. We also know that the saint drove out the old gods and monsters with his faith, but many people may not be familiar with tales of St. Patrick giving chase to demons.

Mystical visions led Patrick back to Ireland, the land that held him captive as a slave in his youth, yet at times the land itself seemed to be against him. In some tales, Patrick made himself an enemy of the old gods, who refused to let go of Ireland and who would confront Patrick with all kinds of evil. During Lent in 441 A.D., for example, Patrick ascended a great mountain in County Mayo in order to fast and do penance. However, according to the seventh-century Irish bishop and biographer Tírechán, in the midst of his solitude, the holy saint was besieged by horrors.

Among the powers of darkness that visited Patrick during this time was a demonic female serpent named Corra or Caoránach. In addition, as night set and Patrick was deep into his prayers, fasting, and penance, demons in the form of blackbirds blocked the sky around him, cawing a demonic song while they destroyed farms and mocked the saint. Patrick first attempted to strike these birds with his crozier, but they would disappear into smoke, then resume their form and mock him and his faith. So Patrick flung holy water while he called out a hymn of praise. The birds retreated but soon came back, harassing fishermen and children on their way.

Finally, Patrick raised his sacred bell. Like today, bells were often used to call people to prayer and the liturgy. He rang out the bell and prayed to God for strength. The demons had never heard such a sound before, and soon they fled in anguish and were replaced by white doves who loudly sang songs of worship. The bell is still in Ireland's national museum, and it is said that Patrick had chased the demons off that mountain once and for all.

The mountain was proclaimed Croagh Patrick, or St. Patrick's Stack, and it bears the nickname "the Reek."[5] To this day, pilgrims gather for Reek Sunday at the end of July to walk barefoot up the rocky slopes of the 2,500-foot-high mountain. Some even start their journey twenty-two miles away at Ballintubber Abbey to walk the ancient pilgrimage route called the *Tochar Padraig*. These tens of thousands of pilgrims reenact a most daring time of Patrick's journey, and the great saint's legacy of penance and prayer lives on in every soul that walks up the sacred mountain.

As word of St. Patrick's many miracles spread, Christians in medieval Europe were especially moved by stories of his vision of the afterlife on a small island on Lough Derg, or Lake of the Cave.

[5] *Reek* is an Irish-English word for "stack."

Pilgrims came from as far away as Hungary and Italy to see this mysterious island cave where the Apostle of Ireland gazed upon the suffering souls in Purgatory. The tale seems tall, but it has impacted poets from Dante to Seamus Heaney, and it even inspired medieval frescoes in the Umbrian hill town of Todi, Italy, not far from Assisi and Orvieto. What captured their imagination, and why did so many people come to this cave?

Patrick arrived at Lough Derg after preaching in the surrounding area of Donegal. The tale goes that the people of Donegal were, at first, hard-hearted and stubborn in their superstitious ways. They especially couldn't believe the Catholic vision of the afterlife and wanted some hard evidence. So Patrick moved to a place of solitude so that he could fast, pray, and do penance for the souls of the people he was trying to convert. While in prayer, Patrick had a vision of Christ calling him to an island cave. When Patrick entered the cave, he was vexed with the images of souls in Purgatory, who called him to pray for them and to do penance for all souls. When Patrick showed this cave to the people and they saw the sufferings that may await them, they begged to be baptized.

Now, in pre-Christian Ireland, there were several caves that were thought to be passages to the underworld. So, in a sense, this miracle "baptized" the old ways of Ireland into the Christian view of the world and helped the people of Ireland reconcile their past culture with the Christian truth. Regardless, what is now called St. Patrick's Purgatory has been a site of Christian pilgrimage for more than 1,500 years, even through the Penal Times of Ireland, when English law attempted to subdue the Catholic Faith.

Among the most famous visitors to this cave was the Knight Owen, who made his pilgrimage in the twelfth century. Owen had done great violence in warfare and sought to do penance for his sins. However, the local abbot was not too keen to let too many people into the cave. Since St. Patrick's time, the cave had a heavy door and lock installed on it, and only a few could enter, on account of the frightening visions. But Owen would not be deterred from doing penance. For fifteen days, he fasted, prayed, and attended Mass. The abbot at last relented, gave the knight the sacraments, and permitted him to enter the purgatorial cave.

It would take too long to discuss Owen's vision, but he saw quite a few souls and met even the saints and angels who instructed him. Most frighteningly, the knight was visited by demons who tried to use scenes of torture to move him from his faith. As he had been advised, the knight called upon the name of Christ to save himself from the demons and their attacks. After he had survived his time in Purgatory, Owen would spend the rest of his days in penance and peace, and his harrowing tale of tortured souls and reassuring angels brought many more pilgrims after him.

The cave is buried now and has been since 1632. But pilgrims still gather to pray, do penance, and sit and think of where their souls may be headed. As these pilgrims continue to gather, pray, and do penance in the footsteps of St. Patrick, they remind us of the beautiful continuity of the Communion of Saints and the universal truth of the Church.

Priest casting out Ossory Werewolves
somewhere between Ulster and Meath, Ireland

Chapter 5

Christian Werewolves?

EMEMBER WHEN I mentioned St. Christopher having the head of a dog in the Vinica icons? Did that seem *weird* to you? Well, stranger still, that is not the only depiction of Christopher with the head of a dog.

In his eleventh-century biography of the saint, known as a hagiography, Walter von Speyer depicts St. Christopher as a giant, dog-headed man from Canaan who even had a vicious bark. As in similar hagiographies, St. Christopher meets the Christ Child and is converted and baptized, but von Speyer also adds that after his conversion, St. Christopher regains his human appearance and is eventually martyred for his new faith. The Byzantine and Russian Churches likewise depict St. Christopher as a human with a dog head in several icons, in which the haloed saint is usually holding the cross of martyrdom.

So was St. Christopher a giant or a forgotten werewolf saint of the early Christian Church? Not at all, but the origin of these stories is as mysterious as it is fascinating. We still don't know why St. Christopher was depicted as a monster, but there are some theories. The most popular is that there was a misreading between the Latin words *chananaeus* ("Canaanite") and *caninus* ("canine"). However, ancient historians did talk about "cynocephaly," or dog-headedness. Pliny the Elder, an ancient Roman writer, discussed the existence of cynocephaly in a far-off land, and later, the Italian explorer Marco Polo discussed a land of dog-headed men in his travel narratives. Neither had firsthand knowledge of these men with dog heads, but clearly the idea was around before and after the stories of St. Christopher.

However, it's also possible that the Orthodox iconographers were appealing more to symbolism than fact when depicting St. Christopher with the head of a dog. Even in those ancient accounts of cynocephaly, dog-headed men represented the very edges of the world. As Orthodox artist Jonathan Pageau notes, "These iconographic examples show the dog-headed men as representing barbarian foreigners *par excellence,* those living on the edge of the world, the edge of humanity itself."[6] Like giants and other monsters, they represented things beyond the known world. And so the hagiographies and artistic traditions of St. Christopher show the power of Christ to save even the most monstrous and barbaric of men. These tales are the stuff of wonder, and they deeply reflect the Catholic view of seeing God's grace in everything. If even monsters can be saved, then there is hope for everyone!

However, werewolves do indeed occur in Christian legends. The most famous legends concern the Ossory Werewolves in Ireland. Wolves were a real concern in medieval Ireland, so much so that they were eventually hunted to extinction. Wolves were therefore at the center of many Irish tales and legends, and there were even many stories of men who turned themselves into wolves, including a royal line that claimed their origin among such werewolves.

According to Gerald of Wales in his twelfth-century *Topographia Hibernica* (Topography of Ireland), a nameless priest encountered

[6] Jonathan Pageau, "Understanding the Dog-Headed Icon of St-Christopher," *Orthodox Arts Journal,* July 8, 2013, https://orthodoxartsjournal.org/the-icon-of-st-christopher/.

two werewolves while traveling between Ulster and Meath. The priest was resting by a fire in the woods in the company of a young man when a mighty wolf suddenly came from the woods and approached the men. The priest and his companion were terrified, but the wolf immediately spoke: "Rest secure, and be not afraid, for there is no reason you should fear, where no fear is."[7]

Of course, the priest and his companion were astonished. Even in Ireland, wolves weren't given to speech. The priest called out to the wolf and, in the name of the Holy Trinity, commanded the beast not to harm them. The wolf, in reply, gave praise to the Trinity and seemed to give Catholic answers to the priest's questions. When the priest asked how a beast could utter human words, the wolf answered that he and his wife were humans who had been cursed by Natalis, an Irish abbot and saint, after the two had spoken blasphemies. As a result of the curse, they were bound to change into the form of wolves every seven years, but they still possessed their human wits. Now, toward the end of their lives, the woman was lying sick in her wolf form, and they hoped the priest would give consolation and last rites to the dying she-wolf.

The priest agreed to follow the wolf, although he was still afraid. He and the wolf found the she-wolf trembling in pain in a hollow by a tree. She too was in wolf form, but she spoke like a human and even praised God that a priest had been provided. The priest blessed her, but he refused to give her the Eucharist, as he knew that animals could not be given Holy Communion. But both wolves begged him for the Eucharist and reassured the priest that they were human. To show that they were not leading the priest to blasphemy, Gerald reports that the wolf, "using his claw for a hand ... tore off the skin of

[7] Giraldus Cambrensis, *The Topography of Ireland*, trans. Thomas Forester (Cambridge, Ontario: In Parentheses Publications, 2000), 44, https://www.yorku.ca/inpar/topography_ireland.pdf.

the she-wolf, from the head down to the navel, folding it back. Thus she immediately presented the form of an old woman."[8] The priest, now reassured, finally gave Communion to the she-wolf, and the wolf led the priest back to his little fire. In the morning, the wolf led the priest out of the woods and gave him prophecies concerning the future of Ireland (as talking animals are wont to do in Irish myths).

Gerald of Wales treats this story as true and includes some theological deliberations about it. He even appeals to St. Augustine to discuss the possibility of men maintaining their human essence even as their outside appears differently. While his arguments present too deep a discussion for this book of marvelous tales, his writings nevertheless show that people didn't just share these stories for fun (although there is a bit of that as well).

On the other hand, we do not have to presume that this story is true to learn from it. The story of the Ossory Werewolves is unique among monster stories in that the wolves talk and are able to use reason. Under all that fur, they are literally and metaphysically human. Because they are human, they are still made in the image of God, but their sin has altered their appearance. They, like all of us, require grace for physical and spiritual ills. The tale also may be a metaphor for missionary work and evangelization, as it reminds us that no matter the differences between ourselves and other people, we are all made in the image of God and are called to be His children. And while the tale demonstrates how wild and weird the world could be, especially in that time and place, it also shows the joyful grace in daily things, and it reminds us that although the world can be savage and strange, there is grace enough that even werewolves can be redeemed. Our Christian ancestors would therefore have heard in this story many aspects of their faith.

[8] Ibid., 45.

Like many tales of monsters, the Werewolves of Ossory has inspired art and especially illuminated manuscripts. These werewolves are terrifying but also oddly relatable. All these monstrous tales may frighten us, but they also teach us important lessons as they relate human emotions to a monster. In the end, they serve to help us see the power of God even when the world tries to hide it under the guise of evil.

There are other monsters that you can find in modern and medieval myths. While it's unlikely people in any era always took these to be factual, there is one both modern and ancient beast that many still think to be true today.

St. Columba stops the Loch Ness monster.
Scotland, United Kingdom

Chapter 6

St. Columba and the Loch Ness Monster

IN THE DAYS of the internet, a lot of monsters who were once just local legends have now become famous worldwide. These so-called "cryptids" include Sasquatch, an ape-man who haunts the forests of the Pacific Northwest, the chupacabra, a Puerto Rican monster who sucks the blood of goats, and, possibly the most famous, the Loch Ness Monster.

The Loch Ness Monster, who is affectionately called Nessie, is a rumored sea serpent that lives in a small lake in the Scottish Highlands. It has been the fascination of monster hunters, photographers, and documentary filmmakers since at least the 1930s, when local sightings of the monster were reported in newspapers. Since then, thousands of tourists have flocked to Loch Ness every year in hopes of spying the beast. Numerous people have said they have seen it, and some have even claimed to have photographed the creature. However, there is a possibility that an Irish saint encountered Nessie long before these modern sightings.

St. Columba, or Colmcille, was born roughly a century after St. Patrick around the year 521 A.D. Like St. Patrick, he was a missionary saint, and he is often called the Apostle of the Picts, an ancient people in Scotland. Also like St. Patrick, his true life is lost in the mists of legend and myth. However, we can get a glimpse of his life through the works he authored and the monasteries he established.

Most of what we know about St. Columba comes from hagiographies written after his death. One of those is the *Vita Columbae,* which was written in the seventh century by St. Adamnán of Iona (or Eunan). This "Life of St. Columba" is intermixed with tales of miracles and exorcisms, and it gives us much of what we know about the saint. The Venerable Bede also wrote about the life of St. Columba as part of a wider history.

According to these accounts, Columba was baptized by his uncle and educated in the monastic tradition. At the time, as the power of Rome waned, Ireland was becoming a light in the so-called "dark ages." The monasteries had become great centers of learning and art. Each monastery usually had a library and scriptorium where monks would work to copy and illustrate manuscripts, the most famous of which was the magnificent *Book of Kells.* As he was educated in the monastery, Columba learned about famous Irish missionaries. And so at the age of forty-two, inspired by their work and devotion, he set out from Ireland to Scotland, where he would work to convert the people. To help his missionary efforts, he founded a monastery on the island of Iona that would become an important center of Christianity. Then he continued to Scotland, converting people as he met them.

In 565 A.D., St. Columba was traveling with several companions by the River Ness, which flows from Loch Ness, where he encountered some local Picts burying a man who was said to have been killed by a river monster. The residents were clearly frightened of this monster and tried to warn Columba, but the saint is recorded as being "far from being dismayed."[9]

9 "The Life of St. Columba," pt. 2, ch. 28, *CELT: The Corpus of Electronic Texts,* https://celt.ucc.ie/published/T201040/.

St. Columba asked one of his companions, a young man named Lugne Mocumin, to swim across the river and obtain one of the boats on the other side. Lugne did as he was asked without delay and swam to the middle of the stream. But as he swam, the monster woke up and darted at Lugne, mouth open for another meal.

All but Columba were terrified at the sight of the monster. The saint raised his hand, made the sign of the cross, and commanded the beast, "Thou shalt go no further, nor touch the man; go back with all speed."[10] At this, the monster was pulled back like it had hooks on its sides. It screamed and fled from the holy man. The people who witnessed this miracle were amazed and converted.

As you can see from this story, St. Columba encountered the monster on the river and not at Loch Ness. Still, the story of a monstrous creature downriver from Loch Ness is something the legend's believers point to when supporting the existence of the famous lake monster. And it is exciting to think that the first record of the Loch Ness Monster goes back more than a thousand years.

Now, Celtic folklore and mythology are full of sea monsters, including the Oilliphéist, a fearsome sea serpent who lurks in many bodies of water across the Isles. This was likely the creature referenced in the tale of St. Columba, as a similar story also occurs in the life of St. Patrick. In the legends about St. Patrick's Purgatory, discussed in chapter 4, Patrick had to contend with an ancient Oilliphéist named Caoránach, the mother of monsters, on Lough Derg before finding the cave with the visions of Purgatory. This worm-like monster was large enough that she would come upon shore to eat cattle. Many feared Caoránach, but St. Patrick was known to have chased away many dark beasts and demons, so he went to Lough Derg and banished the monster from the land. Other tales

[10] Ibid.

say St. Patrick successfully slew the slithering monster, but popular accounts say that Caoránach still lurks in Lough Derg to this day. If she does, no doubt the faith of the various churches and chapels keeps her from harming anyone else.

As in past centuries, these stories of watery monsters are fun to tell, and some of us still believe them. I'm not sure if there is an ancient monster in Loch Ness — I remain skeptical even though I do believe in the supernatural — still, it's a fascinating story, and there may be more to it if you also believe in timeless monsters and spiritual entities.

Aleister Crowley is another figure in the lore of Loch Ness. Called the wickedest man in England, Crowley was obsessed with the occult and believed himself to be a magician and prophet. He also delighted in the negative attention these interests brought to him. Although he might be thought of as a bit of a troll, Crowley was certainly egotistical and self-serious enough to practice his dark rites.

In 1899, Crowley purchased Boleskine House, which sits on the east side of Loch Ness. Even before Crowley purchased the spacious, eighteenth-century house, there were rumors of hauntings and curses surrounding Boleskine, and this reputation, as well as the remoteness of the area, no doubt attracted Crowley. For you see, Crowley wanted to summon demons in order to bind them, an occult ritual that required intense preparation. Crowley was in the midst of his six months of preparation, and he had even begun the ritual, when he was suddenly called to business in Paris. According to local legend, Crowley never completed the ritual; thus the demons had been summoned but never banished.

It seems far-fetched, but when we consider that Crowley was summoning demons at the turn of the twentieth century, mere decades before the number of monster sightings went up in Loch Ness, it all seems rather curious. Could the infamous occultist have summoned the same beast that had originally been banished by St. Columba?

Now, if you're a believer in the Loch Ness Monster, I'm not suggesting that Nessie is a demon. What I think these stories truly demonstrate is how, despite our wonders of science and technology, the world remains strange and mysterious for us, and we continue to be inspired by its weirdness.

Chapter 7

Do You Believe in Monsters?

E'VE DISCUSSED JUST a few saintly encounters with mythical beasts. There are many more stories where these come from, and the lives of the discussed saints could fill libraries. The early and medieval Christian imagination included the possibility that these monsters were real. Demons were assumed to be real.

So, do you believe in monsters? About fifty percent of Americans believe in ghosts and demons,[11] but I am unaware of a poll on how many believe in monsters. And while some of you may believe in cryptids, it's doubtful you've had an active fear of monsters lately. However, we do not need to believe in supernatural beasts to be delighted by these tales of saints and monsters.

Then as now, monsters are an allegory for the edge of the known world. In this sense, to echo Chesterton, we have always had a sense of the monster as a terrifying unknown. Horror movies and stories still attract audiences, as they allow us to explore that part of us that hungers for the supernatural and the mysterious. And we need monster stories to help us understand our fears.

If the monster is an allegory for our fears of the unknown, ancient monster-slaying heroes are a helpful illustration of how

[11] Jaimie Ballard, "About Half of Americans Believe Ghosts and Demons Exist," *YouGov*, October 30, 2020, https://today.yougov.com/society/articles/32807-ghosts-demons-exist-poll-data.

humanity can conquer fear, and the stories of the saints demonstrate the power of God to banish terror. Whether by the power of the Cross or the might of the lance, God's grace is great enough to slay monsters.

But Christianity also has a unique contribution to the monster mythos: God's grace is able to *redeem* the monster. The tales of St. Christopher and of the Ossory Werewolves show us that even the most monstrous of creatures is not beyond God's grace, and they demonstrate the fundamental truth that sometimes a person needs to be loved before we can see them as lovable.

All these stories force us to consider: If even a monster can be saved, how much more hope do we get to have? If even the dog-headed man can become a saint — if even werewolves can seek out salvation — then nobody in this life is beyond the love of God. If the sin of the world has turned our behavior monstrous, we need only to cry to God to help us remember our humanity and to restore our divine image.

As Catholics in a tumultuous world, in which all faults and sins seem to be broadcasted to the public, we should be especially delighted to hear this message. We may not have to ride a horse to fight monsters, and we may never encounter a penitent beast, but we will face terrifying unknowns. And these terrifying unknowns are simply a call to faith and adventure.

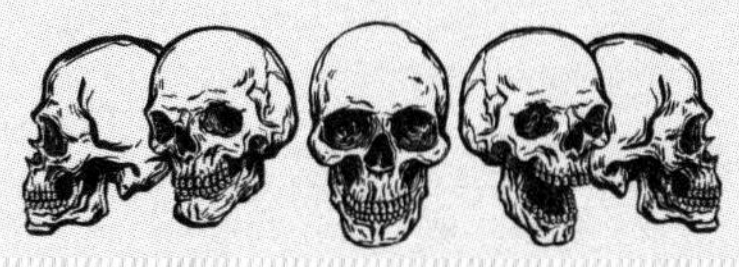

Part 2

Memento Mori: The Church Faces Death

"Our whole life is nothing but a race towards death, in which no one is allowed to stand still for a little space, or to go somewhat more slowly, but all are driven forwards with an impartial movement, and with equal rapidity."

— St. Augustine, *City of God*, 13.10[12]

"Remembering one's death is an absolutely essential aspect of the Christian life, not only because it helps us to live well, but also because it helps us to remember what Christ has done for us."

— Sr. Theresa Aletheia Noble, FSP[13]

NE DAY, YOU and I will die. It's not something we like to think about in modernity, but it is an inescapable reality we all must face. While science and technology have given us longer lifespans, we still have to accept the difficult truth that death is something every person has to contend with.

For early Christians, death was one of the expected outcomes of following Christ. If Jesus Himself had to die, how could it be different for anybody who follows Him? Christ had even promised His first disciples, and other Christians, that martyrdom was a likely outcome

12 In *Nicene and Post-Nicene Fathers, First Series*, vol. 2, trans. Marcus Dods, ed. Philip Schaff (Buffalo, NY: Christian Literature Publishing Co., 1887); revised and edited for *New Advent* by Kevin Knight, available at https://www.newadvent.org/fathers/120113.htm.

13 Theresa Aletheia Noble, *Remember Your Death: A Memento Mori Journal* (Boston: Pauline Books, 2018), 4.

for those preaching the Faith. "Behold," Jesus warned, "I send you out as sheep in the midst of wolves" (Matt. 10:16). However, Jesus also promised the apostles that they would gain eternal life: "He who finds his life will lose it, and he who loses his life for my sake will find it" (Matt. 10:39). So early Christians had a unique view of death; for them, death was not the end but the fulfillment of God's mission.

And so the early martyrs lived lives of holy heroism and faced their own deaths with supernatural fortitude. These martyred heroes were so celebrated that their tombs, relics, and places of martyrdom were made into sacramental touchstones for each new generation of Christians.

Because Christ had promised a future resurrection for all who lost their lives while following Him, Christians found hope as they mourned the dead, who were not gone for good but were merely waiting for the time when Christ would call the living and the dead to Him. From this perspective, the dead weren't just trash to be disposed of and forgotten; they were to be honored and respected as they waited with us for the resurrection. And so Christians buried their dead and prayed for the souls of the departed.

This attitude toward death would intensify during the age of the Black Plague, when Europe lost up to fifty percent of its population. Entire families and villages were completely wiped out as wave after wave of illness swept through the land. Death was everywhere, and it was unavoidable. Those who survived the plague themselves were often still victim to extreme tragedy and loss as they watched their loved ones and neighbors suffer and die, and as religious and lay people meditated on death, they turned to art and religion to process and express their reality. This meditation took on a larger dimension and would be formalized as the practice of *memento mori*, which translates to "remember [your] death" and entails contemplating the inevitability and universality of death in order to enrich your own life.

The idea behind *memento mori* is that if this life is limited, and the next life is eternal, then contemplating death would lead you to live a fuller life. *Memento mori* also called for considering and meditating on Christ's horrific Passion and death in order to bring the faithful soul closer to its Savior. Such contemplation aimed to inspire the Christian to live a life more like Christ's, to engender gratitude for His loving and salvific sacrifice, and to cause us to consider what it means for our own inevitable death.

Meditating on death was especially emphasized in monastic life. Monks and nuns could often be found meditating on death while gazing at the skull of a long-passed brother or sister. This practice was considered essential for conforming one's life to Christ and for keeping all things in perspective.

Memento mori also inspired art and literature. In paintings and sculptures, death was depicted as a cloaked skeleton who was often interrupting people's daily activities to lead them to their final destination. Such works inspired a new form of art called the *Danse Macabre,* the dance of death. Once again, death was depicted as a skeleton, but now he held hands with nobles, clergy, and peasants in a jovial dance that led departed people toward eternity. Often, death was not just leading the dance but was even playing rebecs or flutes to help the passing souls find their rhythm. *Danse Macabre* emphasized the universality of death, showing that all of us had to accept the dance of death eventually. During the Plague, this dance of death could be found carved into tombstones or painted onto church walls across Christendom. While still striking, the dance of death was seen as a happy reality because it meant that the souls of the departed were on their way to meet their Maker.

These Catholic meditations and depictions of death always had hope and joy at their core. Christ had defeated sin and death by His life, death, and Resurrection, and our Christian ancestors believed that while death was indeed inevitable, so indeed was the final, future victory when souls would be united to their bodies and all would meet their Creator. "The last enemy to be destroyed is death" (1 Cor. 15:26), proclaimed St. Paul. This verse is still found in cemeteries across the world and is a foundational doctrine for countless believers.

Death is never an easy subject, but it is much less frightening, and it can even be beautiful and joyful, when we consider and prepare for it. It is important to remember this perspective as we discuss the many ways Catholics of the past honored the dead.

Capuchin Crypt
Rome, Italy

Chapter 1

Ossuaries: Chapels Made of Bones

"And he said to me, 'Son of man, can these bones live?' And I answered, 'O Lord God, thou knowest.' Again he said to me, 'Prophesy to these bones, and say to them, O dry bones, hear the word of the Lord. Thus says the Lord God to these bones: Behold, I will cause breath to enter you, and you shall live.' "

— Ezekiel 37:3–5

HIS IMAGE FROM Ezekiel of dry bones receiving the breath of life is a striking depiction of what the resurrection of the dead might look like, and it has inspired countless Western artists in their attempts to imagine and portray what exactly will happen at the resurrection. Artistic renderings of bones rising from the dead are therefore found not only on tombs and in cemeteries throughout the world, but also in the art of spectacular cathedrals, monasteries, churches, and chapels.

Now imagine going on a pilgrimage to an old city like Rome, Paris, or Lima, or maybe even to a quiet monastery in the Czech countryside. You are there to admire the stunning art and architecture that seem to surround you — and to pray in holy silence as you reflect on these masterful testaments to the great work of God. You soon learn, however, that all these streets and churches have another layer, literally and figuratively. Below the beautiful buildings is the crypt, where the dead are buried in sacred ground. The dead are just as much a part of the city as the living, although we often forget that strange fact. However, taking the time to visit these places beneath our churches will yield some delightful surprises.

There are also some places that may frighten the unsuspecting pilgrim: chapels with walls and altars made of human skulls, chandeliers composed of bones, and columns and pyramids made of stacked femurs. These sacred spaces made of bones are known as ossuaries, from the Latin word for bone, *os*. For modern pilgrims, ossuaries may seem like spooky Catholic Halloween decorations or the work of dark wizards or modern metalheads, but they are instead the faithful creations of monks and artists who built them to be places of deep sacredness and reminders of our own death. Indeed, ossuaries are the purest expression of *memento mori*.

Let's look at one of the most famous ossuaries, which is located in the Capuchin crypt beneath Santa Maria della Concezione dei Cappuccini (St. Mary of the Conception and the Capuchins) in Rome. The church that houses the ossuary had been a dream of the Capuchin Cardinal Antonio Marcello Barberini, a member of a princely family and the brother of Pope Urban VIII. He found land on Via Veneto near his family's palace and assigned Fra Michele da Bergamo, a Capuchin friar, as the architect for his church, which was to be dedicated to Mary's Immaculate Conception. In honor of the Capuchins' spiritual father, construction began on the feast of St. Francis of Assisi in 1626 and was completed in 1631.[14] The church is

[14] "Chiesa di Santa Maria della Concezione," Turismo Roma, accessed March 17, 2024, https://www.turismoroma.it/it/luoghi/chiesa-di-santa-maria-della-concezione.

beautiful and hosts countless works of art by some of the greatest artists Rome had to offer.

As the Capuchins settled into their new church, they couldn't simply leave behind their departed brothers. The Capuchins were and still are devoted in their continuous prayers for the dead, especially those within their order. They kept their deceased brothers' bones together in the sacred ground beneath their old church, and the names of each deceased friar or benefactor were kept in books for daily prayer. The dead were just as much a part of their ministry as the living. So they had to move their dead.

While it may seem strange to us today to exhume bodies and move them across town, we need to understand the reality our Christian ancestors faced. A common problem with burial grounds throughout Christendom was that there was only so much room for the dead. Everyone must die, and they must be given a Christian burial, but what do you do when you run out of space? Many cemeteries would therefore move bodies once they decomposed to bones. The newly dead would now have a place to be buried, and the skeletal remains were still given a respectable re-burial as they awaited the resurrection.

The Capuchin Crypt was a special place: not only was it sacred ground because it was part of a church, but it contained soil from Jerusalem. So members and benefactors of the order considered it especially sacred, and in a short time, the crypt had more bones than it could handle. That is when the ossuary began to take shape.

The ossuary is a decoration of bones from the remains of four thousand monks. The chapels include skulls, passageways lined with finger bones, and the remains of monks in their robes situated as if in prayer. Who designed it is in some dispute. One popular source has the architect Fra Michele da Bergamo as the original designer and artist behind the arrangement of bones,[15] but I can't confirm a direct source for this suggestion, and other accounts name other artists starting the project. What seems most likely is that the bone decorations took shape shortly after the move, and later generations added onto them. But we know that the ossuary was a popular sight only a few years after its construction because many travelers from at least the early eighteenth century on have written accounts of the ossuary.

For as long as it has been open to the public, the ossuary has frightened tourists and inspired pilgrims. American author Nathaniel Hawthorne, for example, called the crypt "ugly and grotesque"[16] in one of his novels and wrote:

> In the side walls of the vaults are niches where skeleton monks sit or stand, clad in the brown habits that they wore in life, and labelled with their names and the dates of their decease.[17]

Mark Twain likewise was disturbed by what he witnessed in the ossuary, whose "picturesque horrors" he described in his book *The Innocents Abroad* as "grotesque" and "ghastly."[18]

But if you believe in the resurrection of the dead promised by Christ, or even if you know about it, you can see the ossuary in a light

15 Michele Sanvico, "Capuchin Crypt," retrieved March 17, 2024, *Italian Writer's Guide to Unknown Rome*, http://www.italianwriter.it/Unknown-Rome/Guide_to_Unknown_Rome_10_CapuchinCrypt.asp.

16 Nathaniel Hawthorne, *The Marble Faun*, vol. 1 (Boston: Ticknor and Fields, 1861), ch. 21; available at *Project Gutenberg*, https://www.gutenberg.org/files/2181/2181-h/2181-h.htm.

17 Ibid.

18 Mark Twain, *The Innocents Abroad* (Hartford: American Publishing Company, 1869), ch. 28; available at *Project Gutenberg*, https://www.gutenberg.org/files/3176/3176-h/3176-h.htm.

that was missed by two of my favorite novelists. The first thing a visitor to the crypt will see is a painting of Christ raising Lazarus from the dead. This image is, of course, framed by various parts of the human skeleton, but it shows us that the purpose of the ossuary is not simply to disturb us for no reason.

In St. John's Gospel, Lazarus was a friend of Jesus who had fallen ill and died. Jesus was away at the time but knew His friend had died and said, "Our friend Laz'arus has fallen asleep, but I go to awake him out of sleep" (11:11). As He promised, Jesus returned to raise Lazarus from the dead. However, Christ also spoke of the resurrection that everyone would experience. "He who believes in me, though he die, yet shall he live" (11:25), Jesus told His disciples before raising Lazarus.

So the raising of Lazarus is the ideal image for the entrance to any Catholic burial space, but it's quite appropriate for the ossuary beneath Santa Maria della Concezione, as it provides our first hint at the themes of resurrection and death that decorate the chapels. Lazarus was raised from the dead although he had been in the tomb for days. These bones buried in this tomb in Rome likewise belonged to people who had faith that their resurrection would happen no matter how long they waited.

Toward the end of the crypt is another call to *memento mori*. At a chapel built from skulls emerges three skeletons clothed in the brown robes of the Capuchin order. Each skeleton holds an item to represent death and, as if the bones could talk, a sign proclaims in five languages, "What you are now, we once were; what we are now, you shall be." And so even now these monks call us to pray and meditate about our ultimate fate and what it means for how we'll live today.

The Capuchin Crypt has a special place in my heart because I first visited as a tourist but walked out as a pilgrim. I was a student in Rome, and I wanted to see something spooky. I gawked at the chapels made of skulls and the decorations made from thigh bones and vertebrae; meanwhile a man prayed a Rosary in the silent, sacred space. I wasn't expecting to find myself praying for these long-dead friars, but suddenly I was, and I was struck by that final sign from the bones: "What you are now, we once were; what we are now, you shall be."

When I left the crypt, I found myself aware of my own mortality in a way I never considered. However, it was a peaceful and even joyful feeling. At that moment, I thought about how the bones I just prayed for would one day be reunited with their souls, and they would be my friends and brothers in eternal life. We were divided by time, life, language, and even culture, but we were also united in so many ways that I already felt like these long-deceased friars were now among the many friends I had met on my travels. My meditations allowed me to realize on a deeper level that all of us, living and dead, were united to each other by our Creator and Redeemer. While death was part of the universal human experience, it did not have to be the final word.

That moment inspired many more visits to many other ossuaries, but it also made me more devout in praying for the dead. I didn't even know the term *memento mori* at the time, but it had already changed my life. That moment of prayer and meditation has led to my regularly praying for the dead, supporting local cemeteries, and seeking a way to tell the stories of our predecessors. And I'm far from the only person who had an unexpected spiritual experience in the ossuary. Many visitors go there and find peace and clarity, and they later return to see if they can repeat that experience. There are also the fortunate pilgrims who are prepared for the confrontation with mortality that these places offer to us, and so they are able to pray and contemplate in a way I had not when I first visited an ossuary.

If the Capuchin Crypt were just a sideshow attraction, I don't think it would have as many intentional and repeat visitors decade after decade. Instead, the spirituality of the place and the invitation of *memento mori* keeps people returning. Yes, some visitors will only experience the place as a frightening specter, but many more will find a place of serene reflection in these chapels made of bones. And as such places of deep spiritual reflection disappear from our culture, I take great comfort in the Capuchin friars keeping this sacred crypt open to all pilgrims, the intentional and unintentional alike.

A Pilgrimage Surrounded by Bones

The ossuary of Santa Maria della Concezione dei Cappuccini was not the first ossuary in the world, but it might be the most famous and most influential. It often shows up on must-see lists and tours, and it has been visited by many famous writers and artists who increase the fame of the ossuary with their vivid descriptions. But there are other ossuaries in Italy (such as San Bernardino alle Ossa in Milan) and in other countries in Europe that are worth visiting, and they are far less popular than the Roman Capuchin Crypt, which means that these quiet and often-empty ossuaries are usually better places for prayer and meditation.

In the small Czech town of Kutna Hora, an hour outside of Prague, is one such ossuary that was inspired by Santa Maria della Concezione. In the Gothic-baroque chapel of All Saints, right in the middle of an ancient cemetery and Cistercian abbey, is the Sedlec Ossuary, a true wonder of central Europe. The beautiful, baroque design of the ossuary is complemented by lavish decorations in bones, including a grand chandelier that is made from every bone found in the human body, with skulls serving as luminaires. There are also cherubs holding human skulls while blowing their horns, and, to demonstrate the great artistry involved in arranging bones, there are images of the Cross, a chalice, and a pyramid all made of bones.

Sedlec Ossuary
Kutna Hora, Czech Republic

It is estimated that the bones of the Sedlec Ossuary come from the remains of between forty thousand and seventy thousand people, scores more than what can be found in Rome's Capuchin Crypt. Also, Sedlec is a much more recent creation compared to Rome's famous ossuary. We know who created the ossuary and when, in part because the artist, František Rint, left his signature and the date of 1870 on the wall of the ossuary using arm bones and smaller finger bones.

The origins of Sedlec Ossuary are older than the elaborate decoration of bones that currently exists. The All Saints' Church that contains the ossuary was once the cemetery church of Sedlec Abbey, a Cistercian monastery founded in 1142. This abbey was an important center for learning and spirituality, but it also became wealthy after silver was discovered nearby. Local legend also says that around 1278, the abbot of Sedlec made a pilgrimage to the Holy Land and returned with earth from Golgotha, the place where Christ was crucified.[19] As with the Capuchin Crypt in Rome, the Sedlec cemetery therefore became a very desirable final resting place for the monks and the laity.

Sedlec Abbey also suffered many calamities that further necessitated a large cemetery. Plague, war, famine, and political instability would rock Czech lands for centuries. The monastery itself was destroyed and looted during the Hussite Wars in 1421, and it would see more fires, debt, and strife until it was finally dissolved in 1783 by order of the Holy Roman Emperor. The monastery grounds then became the property of the noble Schwarzenberg family, who had the familiar problem of having too many bones for their small cemetery church.

[19] "Ossuary Sedlec: The Cemetery Church of All Saints," The Roman Catholic Parish of Kutná Hora, Sedlec, https://www.sedlec.info/en/ossuary/history/.

The cemetery church's interior was restored and decorated in the early eighteenth century. However, the bones were merely piles when the Schwarzenbergs hired woodcarver František Rint to decorate the church crypt with the bones in 1870. Whoever designed the macabre decorations of bones, Rint had the task of putting it all together, and his work feels like it was always meant to be in this baroque setting. Rint even paid tribute to his patrons by creating the House of Schwarzenberg coat of arms out of skeletal remains in extraordinary detail.

After its completion, Sedlec Ossuary was visited and admired by curious travelers, and it was widely photographed and painted. Unfortunately, the ossuary would suffer from neglect in the twentieth century: bones were stolen, the chapel was abandoned, and the ossuary might have been forgotten altogether were it not for its popularity on the internet and the work of the local Catholic parish. Now, it is among the most popular attractions in the Czech Republic, and it is thankfully undergoing a full restoration.

The hundreds of thousands of people who visit Sedlec may not know the history or the cultural significance of this place, but they are still affected by the ossuary. No matter your spiritual beliefs, it is a striking and beautiful space that confronts death in a way few will ever experience. Some laugh nervously as they look around, many others are moved to prayer for the dead, but all walk away from Sedlec impacted by its memory.

The two ossuaries I've covered in this chapter receive a lot of attention and traffic, so it can be hard to see these places like previous generations did. Try to imagine, though, people visiting places like these for solitary prayer and contemplation. The lights are low, the shadows of candles dance along the walls, and the only sounds are perhaps the echoing footsteps of monks, the soft click of rosary beads, or a hushed prayer from a fellow pilgrim. You can imagine that such a place would lead to some deep questions and thoughts about your own mortality, while also providing you with a sense of peace and compassion. It's possible to get this experience at some of the smaller, lesser-known ossuaries (see part five of this book). Still, you can also understand this feeling even on the busiest of days in an ossuary.

The spiritual experience of ossuaries is intentional. Like many Catholic churches and chapels, ossuaries were designed by devout artists and craftsmen to remind you of another world. They transport you from the quotidian rhythms of daily life to moments filled with eternity. They inspire us to prayer and reflection as we come to terms with our mortality and challenge ourselves to use the time we have wisely. Each ossuary is a spiritual pilgrimage that calls us to truly examine the lives we're leading and to consider what we would want to leave behind.

Ossuaries aren't for everyone, and some of you may react like Nathaniel Hawthorne or Mark Twain did. However, you can still see these sacred chapels as places of deep contemplation where we confront mortality and examine how we can live our own lives. I think that is why people like me make many return visits to these bone churches and why a new generation is securing their preservation. If you can, though, try to experience these places as quietly as possible, and ask God for the grace to find the peace that many people feel after visiting these unique chapels.

Capuchin Mummies
Brno, Czechia

Chapter 2

Christian Mummies?

MUMMIES HAVE A fascinating place in history and pop culture. People in the West have long been intrigued by Egyptian mummies in particular, and many of those preserved bodies have made their way to museums and private collections. Of course, the mummy has also been the horror antagonist in multiple films.

Mummies and mummification go deeper than the bandage-wrapped and supposedly curse-filled bodies of Egyptian royals, though. Several ancient cultures on multiple continents practiced intentional mummification in some form, including, for example, the ancient Chinchorro mummies of modern Chile, which predate the Egyptian mummies by more than two thousand years. There have also been cases of accidental mummification, when bodies are preserved unintentionally through the environment of their burial space.

As far as I know, there is no long-established tradition for intentional mummification in Western Christianity. Also, unlike with the werewolves in chapter 5, I know of no ancient hagiographies that speak of Christian mummies asking for blessings. However, there are many instances of accidental mummies being created in Christian tombs. These preserved bodies were discovered decades or centuries after they were buried, and usually by accident, when coffins and tombs were opened for routine maintenance or to move the bones.

Christians have been burying their dead beneath churches for centuries, either in tombs or simply in the ground of a crypt. These places not only provided a location for the deceased to await the resurrection, but they also gave the faithful a space to visit, remember, and pray for the dead. Crypts were also home to relics and tombs of saints, making them all the more desirable for interring the dead as they gave families comfort to see their departed loved ones in the midst of holy company. Many church crypts featured just tombs and markers noting the names of the dearly departed, but they could also be as elaborate as the ossuaries we have already examined. Most of the time, however, crypts were simply peaceful and prayerful places without any hint of the unusual. But it turns out that some of these crypts and tombs provided the perfect environment for preserving bodies. Places like St. Michan's Church in Dublin, for example, built their old crypts out of limestone, which created a cool, dry air perfect for accidental mummification.

The mummified bodies of St. Michan's have been attracting tourists for at least a century. Even a young Bram Stoker is said to have visited the burial vaults beneath St. Michan's Church (although I couldn't find a direct source to prove this claim).[20] Among the St. Michan's mummies are a man believed to be a crusader and a nun whose remains are four hundred years old. Their facial features are still discernable, and if it weren't for the tattered remains of their clothes and coffins, it would be hard to believe that these were the remains of people who had been dead for centuries.

[20] Genevieve Fitzgerald, "Supernatural Dublin — St. Michan's Church," *Dublin.ie*, retrieved March 27, 2024, https://dublin.ie/live/stories/supernatural-dublin-st-michans-church/.

St. Michan's is a longstanding curiosity that is worth a visit if you're in Dublin. However, the presentation of the mummies can feel divorced from the Catholic roots of the church and its burial space. In such a busy and evocative place, it can be hard to find deep, spiritual meaning. This crypt still provides opportunities for us to reflect on death, but this significance is easier to find in another crypt.

The Capuchin Church of the Finding of the Holy Cross lies not far from the central market of Brno, Czechia. The church features a single nave, simple baroque decorations, and images of saints.[21] Underneath its beautiful facade is a crypt, but unlike the Capuchin crypt in Rome, this one is not made of bones. Instead, it holds the mummified remains of multiple friars and a few of their benefactors. The stone and chimneys of the church circulated air and kept the temperature and humidity low, and as a result, these mummies are so well preserved that you can make out their facial features and expressions.[22] Like other places we discuss in this section of the book, Brno's Capuchin Crypt is featured in many lists of "dark tourism," and your average guide will cast it as a disturbing and morbid place to visit. On the other hand, the modern Capuchins present this crypt as a place of *memento mori* where visitors can practice prayer and contemplation.

When the pilgrim enters the Capuchin Crypt, he will see a sign similar to the one in Rome's ossuary, declaring, "As you are now, we once were; as we are now, you shall be." This familiar reminder is found in many Christian crypts, even ones without mummies or

[21] Kapucíni v Brně, "Church of the Finding of the Holy Cross," accessed March 27, 2024, https://hrobka.kapucini.cz/subdom/hrobka/index.php/en/history-of-the-capuchins-in-brno/church-of-the-finding-of-the-holy-cross.

[22] Ibid.

bones, and it serves to remind pilgrims that all of us must face our death one day. It also causes us to pause and recognize the humanity in these mummified remains.

It becomes obvious to any visitor to the Capuchin Crypt that Brno's modern Capuchin brothers keep this place as an act of love and as a ministry. For the living Capuchins, these dead brothers and benefactors are people to be loved and prayed for. The names of the deceased were all recorded in books for prayer and Mass intentions, and the benefactors and lay workers are named and given short biographies on signs throughout the crypt. These benefactors were also buried in coffins elaborately decorated with religious paintings of a crucifix or *danse macabre* skulls, and today their mummified remains can be seen beneath a modern glass top.

The friars, however, as an act of poverty, were only buried in the bare dirt, but they are now displayed in the crypt, where many visitors witness the bare mummies wearing their brown religious robes and holding crosses. The names of the priests and brothers of the order are not recorded in their simple burial space, and today they are lined up anonymously in the crypt before a crucifix. Yet these humble souls are still displayed with great dignity, as they were lovingly arranged by one of the Capuchin friars, Zeno Diviš, who also wrote the crypt's first historical guide in the early twentieth century.[23] Brother Diviš took great care to give each body a place of dignity that also stressed the importance of remembering one's death and praying for the departed. Yes, the mummified remains of long-dead friars can be shocking, but the fraternal love that went into their care is obvious, and one leaves with a feeling

[23] Ibid.

best described by a friend who said to me, "It's shocking, tender, strange, and comforting all at the same time."

As you exit the Capuchin Crypt, you see one last reminder, a baroque angel pointing to a stone plaque that reads, *Sic Transit Gloria Mundi* ("Thus passes the glory of the world"). This plaque reminds us of the impermanence of all things, from our very lives to the empires and orders that stand in our time. This message was so impactful that occupying Nazis ordered the removal of the statue and plaque.[24] Apparently, the idea of the transience of all earthly things offended the fascists, who imagined they were starting a millennial Reich. But this message, along with the stark reminder of death in the crypt, calls us to know that everything is but a blip in God's eternity, and it reminds us that we should concern our thoughts with the things of eternity. So while the reminder that all things must end is displeasing to some, it is a comfort for many more people who make their way through the crypt and confront these realities.

Ars Moriendi: *The Art of a Good Death*

The Christian mummies in places like the Capuchin Crypt are an invitation to *memento mori,* to meditate on the end of our lives and the end of the world and what that reality might mean for the rest of our days. The Capuchin order also wanted to remind visitors of another Catholic tradition, *ars moriendi,* or "the art of dying well." The art of dying well is concerned with having a "good death," wherein a soul is

[24] Ibid.

reconciled to God and neighbor, and the family is cared for after the death of their loved one. A good death meant that you had led a good life and had prepared yourself for death. It also meant that death would not be frightening or surprising but something that one would welcome as the gateway into eternity.

Members of religious orders have long considered the art of dying well, and the art was especially emphasized in the seventeenth century, when the Capuchin Crypt in Brno was built. The bloody century had featured massive wars, plague, and great political change, so it became more crucial for everyone to practice the art of dying well as they experienced death in a visceral way everyday. It's always important to consider our death, but it becomes something people naturally contemplate more when they are faced with it in such a way. To that end, theologian St. Robert Bellarmine wrote the widely read book *The Art of Dying Well* (*De Arte Bene Moriendi*) in 1620. This book was translated and printed across Europe and had a profound impact on the wider culture.

St. Robert Bellarmine stressed that considering how to have a good death should lead us to live life more fully. As the saint said, "A good death depends upon a good life."[25] Like *memento mori, ars moriendi* is not about despair in the face of death but serves as an encouragement to use our remaining time wisely. According to St. Robert, a good life starts with dying to the world: "Now, to live well, it is necessary, in the first place, that we die to the world before we die in the body."[26] Dying to the world means loving God alone above everything else. While we can admire beautiful things, we can't love them more than people, and we can't love anyone more than God.

[25] St. Robert Bellarmine, *The Art of Dying Well*, trans. John Dalton (Manchester, NH: Sophia Institute Press, 2021), 5.

[26] Ibid., 8.

St. Robert Bellarmine believed that once someone has died to the world, he can be more open to the spiritual things that truly fulfill us, especially partaking of the sacraments, praying fervently, practicing charity, detaching from the world, giving generously, and disciplining the body through fasting. All of these were to be practiced over a lifetime in order to prepare the soul to meet Christ after death. In short, the art of dying well was learning to distinguish between momentary things and everlasting things.[27]

I can't prove that any of the first Brno Capuchins buried beneath Holy Cross read St. Robert Bellarmine's book. Unfortunately, the Capuchin's vast library in Brno is only open to select researchers. However, the book was influential and spoke to an idea that was already embraced by the order: by learning to die well, we can learn to truly live well.

The Capuchins still strive to live their lives in the spirit of St. Francis, taking vows of poverty so that they can help those around them. As members of a religious order, they saw their spiritual and corporeal works as the ideal for living well and dying well. Thus, it was an honor for them to be buried simply and without a coffin in the sacred church ground. That the same church ground also mummified them is a happy accident, but one embraced by later Capuchins who saw another opportunity to meditate on temporary and eternal things.

Few of us will live like seventeenth-century monks. And even fewer of us will have a grave that is widely visited. All the same, every one of us has to contend with the inevitability of death and what kind of legacy we will leave behind when it's our time to go, and we are also called to live in preparation for meeting Christ.

[27] Ibid., 125.

There are many ways to learn and practice *memento mori* and *ars moriendi*. Reading classic books like St. Robert Bellarmine's or modern books like Sr. Theresa Aletheia Noble's *Memento Mori* are good places to start, combined with prayer and daily meditation. But I can also speak from experience when I say that visiting places like Brno's Capuchin crypt is also an effective way to start learning these important Catholic practices. When I look back on my visit to this crypt, the feeling I remember most was tenderness, as the love of the modern Capuchins for their departed brothers and benefactors was so clear to me. I was there to pray and meditate while walking through the crypt, and it really was the most natural thing to stop and pray for just about every person I saw there. These were my brothers and sisters in Christ, and I truly felt that as I was praying for my fellow Catholics, they too were praying for me. Their bodies were mummified, but I believe that they will still rise on Judgment Day, and that gave me a great deal of comfort.

There are other crypts where natural mummification takes place, but not all of them will be as focused on the spiritual roots of the burial space. If you ever decide to visit such a crypt, I've found that the Capuchins, who host several such crypts of Christian mummies, seem to do the best job at presenting the spiritual dimension of this phenomenon (see part five of this book). But you may view mummified monks differently. Death is always a heavy subject, and seeing its consequences is bound to inspire a lot of varied feelings. However, I hope that at the very least you can appreciate the historical and cultural roots of these special crypts where the dead are accidentally preserved and see the beauty many people find in these places that are so easily dismissed as merely morbid or dark.

The Christian mummies found beneath churches worldwide may have been unintentional, but there is still much to glean from their existence. While these mummies can be explained by science and environment, we also need to recognize that sometimes there are also unintentionally preserved bodies that completely defy explanation. These are bodies of the Incorruptibles, whom we'll discuss in the next section. However, keep all we've said about mummification in mind while we explore the unusual miracle of incorruptible saints.

St. Cecilia Marble Statue
Rome, Italy

Chapter 3

The Incorruptibles

S YOU HAVE learned, there can be some immense surprises hiding in Catholic burial spaces. Though the ones we've discussed can be explained, there is one phenomenon that many faithful Catholics regard as miraculous. When a saint's tomb is opened, sometimes people find a body that is so preserved that the saint looks like he or she has fallen asleep or only recently died. These preserved saints are known as the Incorruptibles, and their existence has long been a source of mystery and mysticism.

The Catholic Church considers a body incorrupt when it is free from preservation or embalming techniques but still retains lifelike color, freshness in appearance, and flexibility of its limbs. There also must not be any other explanation for the body's preservation, such as in the crypts we discussed earlier. Unlike the notoriously brittle mummies you might find in an old crypt, incorrupt bodies can also still be moved and repositioned. Even the smell of putrefaction is often absent in these cases.

In the eighteenth century, Prospero Cardinal Lambertini, who would later become Pope Benedict XIV, wrote a work called *De Cadaverum Incorruptione,* which has been the standard for judging if a body is incorrupt. Of course, both curious scientists and religious scholars are interested in the phenomenon of incorruptibility, and so there have been several studies of these saintly bodies. And what they find is as fascinating as it is odd.

Before we get into possible explanations for incorruptibility, let's first describe a few of the Incorruptibles and how they have influenced believers throughout the ages. We should start with Rome, as St. Cecilia is the most famous of incorrupt saints. The patron saint of music and an early martyr in Rome.

St. Cecilia belonged to an upper-class family in Rome in the second century. From an early age, she was dedicated to the Christian Faith and even took a vow of virginity. Despite her vow, however, the future saint's parents arranged for her to be married to a nobleman named Valerian. But Cecilia's dedication and passion helped convert Valerian to the Faith, and he would honor her vow even after their marriage. She also converted Valerian's brother, Tiburtius.

Around 177 A.D., Valerian and Tiburtius were martyred after they refused to renounce their faith. Being a good Christian, Cecilia buried her husband and brother-in-law in some catacombs on the Appian Way, and as a result of her act of mercy, Cecilia was also condemned to be executed. But the executioner did not want to harm the young lady. A less experienced executioner was therefore brought in to kill St. Cecilia in her own home. He struck her neck several times, but he failed to fully decapitate her. The wounded Cecilia lay on her floor with her hands folded in a prayer, and she prayed until she finally died.

Pope Urban I, who had baptized her household, buried St. Cecilia in the catacombs, and popular devotion to this martyr began immediately. Her cult remained strong in subsequent centuries, and a church was built over her home, the place of her martyrdom. In 822, Pope Paschal I moved her body, along with the bodies of her husband, brother-in-law, and other early Church martyrs, to the Basilica of St. Cecilia in Trastevere, Rome.

In 1599, the Cardinal protector of St. Cecilia's Basilica, Cardinal Paolo Emilio Sfondrati, undertook a restoration of his church and also ordered an examination of St. Cecilia's relics. On October 20, he and a group of witnesses gathered as workers uncovered the marble sarcophagus and removed the cypress casket. The casket was in great shape, but nothing could prepare them for what they saw next. Through her silk burial veil, the remains of St. Cecilia were perfectly preserved even centuries after her death.[28]

The body of St. Cecilia appeared in the exact position she was in when she had died. To the amazement of Cardinal Sfrondrati and others, her body was so well preserved that even the wounds around her neck appeared to be fresh. Her incorrupt body drew thousands of pilgrims until she was reinterred on November 22, her feast day. Stefano Maderno, the greatest sculptor of his day, was meanwhile hired to depict St. Cecilia's incorrupt body in a marble statue that still sits in her basilica.[29] Maderno depicted the saint exactly as she was found, and the marks of her martyrdom are obvious even in marble.

There had been incorruptible saints discovered before St. Cecilia, but the discovery of her preserved relics was witnessed and celebrated by many. St. Cecilia was an early martyr and a beloved saint, so her incorruptible state was just one more reason for people to celebrate her holiness. Still, the phenomenon of incorruptibility is not just relegated to ancient history.

In 2023, a potential new case of an incorruptible body was reported. As word spread, pilgrims came from hundreds of miles away to see the preserved body. This time, though, Americans didn't have to fly to Europe; they could simply drive to Missouri.

Sr. Mary Wilhelmina Lancaster, OSB, died in 2019 at the age of ninety-five. As the founder of a religious order, she was buried

[28] Joan Carroll Cruz, *The Incorruptibles* (Charlotte, NC: TAN Books, 2012), 3–4.

[29] Brigitte Hintzen-Bohlen, *Art and Architecture: Rome and the Vatican City*, trans. Peter Barton (Königswinter: Tandem Verlag GmbH, 2005), 423.

on the monastery grounds of the Benedictines of Mary, Queen of Apostles, near Gower, Missouri. Sr. Wilhelmina had been a religious sister since the age of seventeen, and she accomplished much in her decades of religious life. She worked as a schoolteacher and administrator in schools across the East Coast for more than fifty years, then she founded the Benedictines of Mary in 2005 in order to preserve the order's habit and the traditional prayers Benedictine nuns have been singing and praying for centuries. The order she founded is still active: the sisters live the Benedictine life of prayer and work, and they have even recorded several best-selling albums of Gregorian chant and liturgical music.[30]

On April 28, 2023, nearly four years after her death, the sisters of the Benedictines of Mary exhumed the remains of their foundress in order to reinter them into a newly built shrine to St. Joseph. The good foundress had been buried in a simple coffin with no embalming or preservation work done, and so the sisters were expecting to find nothing but bones.[31] The coffin even had a crack down its middle, further exposing her body to moisture. But to the surprise of the gathered sisters, Sr. Wilhelmina's body was intact and seemed to be preserved. Even her religious habit was undamaged.

The sisters further reported, "Not only was her body in a remarkable preserved condition, her crown and bouquet of flowers were dried in place; the profession candle with the ribbon, her crucifix, and

[30] Kelsey Wicks, "Who Was Sister Wilhelmina Lancaster, Whose Body Is Now the Center of Attention in Missouri?" *Catholic News Agency*, May 24, 2023, https://www.catholicnewsagency.com/news/254413/who-was-sister-wilhelmina-lancaster-the-african-american-whose-body-is-potentially-incorrupt.

[31] "More Information about Sr. Wilhelmina," *Benedictines of Mary, Queen of Apostles*, accessed March 29, 2024, https://benedictinesofmary.org/srwilhelmina/.

rosary were all intact."[32] News quickly spread, and the story of Sr. Wilhelmina and her possible incorruptibility was reported in international headlines. Her case is especially significant in Catholic history because if her body is indeed proven to be incorruptible, she will be the first African American woman to be declared incorruptible.[33]

For those who knew her, Sr. Wilhelmina's sanctity was already clear, but now her name and life are known worldwide. For the Benedictines of Mary, Sr. Wilhelmina's preserved habit is especially a wonder. In traditional religious orders, the habit is more than just clothing; it is a sign of a member's vow and a sign of things to come, especially our final end. The habit is also how most laity recognize members of religious orders. And so the seemingly miraculous preservation of Sr. Wilhelmina's habit was especially important to the nuns. As Abbess Cecilia, the current leader of the Benedictines of Mary, said to a reporter, "God is real. He protected that body and that habit to enkindle our faith, to rekindle it, to bring people back to the Faith."[34]

Although she has inspired many, there is currently no open cause for the canonization of Sr. Wilhelmina, and the Vatican has yet to study her remains.[35] So we do not yet know whether or not this phenomenon can be explained or if it is a miracle. For now, though, many are excited about the possibility of an incorruptible saint in rural Missouri, and believers who have witnessed the remains of Sr. Wilhelmina have another reason to hope for the future as we look to

32 Kelsey Wicks, "A Miracle in Missouri? Body of Benedictine Sisters' Foundress Thought to Be Incorrupt," *Catholic News Agency*, May 22, 2023, https://www.catholicnewsagency.com/news/254384/a-miracle-in-missouri-body-of-benedictine-sisters-foundress-thought-to-be-incorrupt.

33 Ibid.

34 Ibid.

35 Hannah Brockhaus, "What Is Incorruptibility? Here's What You Need to Know," May 25, 2023, https://www.catholicnewsagency.com/news/254416/what-is-incorruptibility-here-s-what-you-need-to-know.

the resurrection of the living and the dead, the Final Judgment, and our (hopeful) reunion with Christ in Paradise.

Sometimes parts of a saint are incorrupt, even when they are separated from the rest of the body. These incorrupt pieces are often discovered centuries after the saint's death, when other churches request relics. For example, the tongue of St. John Nepomucene, a fourteenth-century Bohemian priest and martyr, was found to be incorrupt in the eighteenth century. This event was widely celebrated, and a pilgrimage church was built for the incorrupt tongue.[36] Given that St. John was executed for protecting the secrecy of the confessional, it seems almost poetic that his tongue was left preserved. Those devoted to St. John understood from this miracle that the saint was still singing the glory of God.

In some other cases, relics will be removed from an incorrupt body and remain preserved. This was the case with the body of St. Francis Xavier, the famous Jesuit missionary. St. Francis Xavier was an early companion of St. Ignatius of Loyola, the founder of the Jesuits, and he journeyed to places like India and Japan, converting people as he went. After falling ill on his way to China, St. Francis Xavier died on December 3, 1552, at the age of forty-six. St. Francis's companions knew his body would be moved, so they initially buried him in a lonely spot that would be easy to find. They also added lime to his burial spot in order to hasten the body's decomposition so that only bones would need to be transported.[37]

On February 17, 1553, St. Francis's coffin was unearthed to be placed on a ship going to Malacca. Underneath the layer of lime,

[36] "The Impulse and Preparation of the Church," *The Pilgrimage Church of Saint John of Nepomuk at Zelená hora*, accessed March 30, 2024, https://www.zelena-hora.eu/en/the-history/chronology/the-impulse-and-preparation-of-the-church.

[37] Cruz, *The Incorruptibles*, 145.

however, his body was found to still be preserved. His body was then transported to Malacca before it was finally buried in Goa, India. Over the next 150 years, the body of St. Francis was examined by doctors and witnessed by countless pilgrims.[38] All attest to the incorruptibility of St. Francis Xavier.

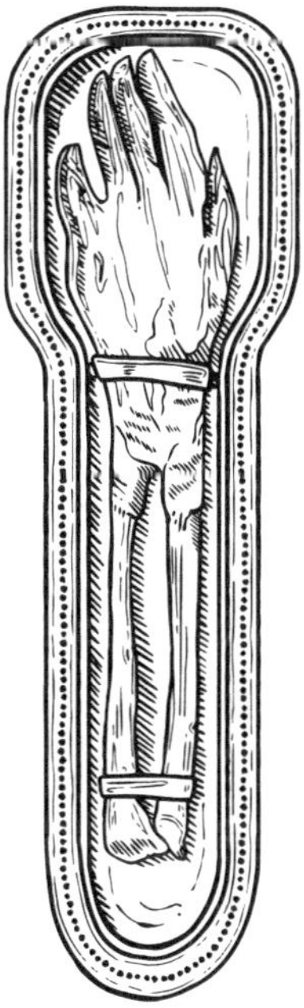

In 1614, Rome's Jesuit church, il Gesù, requested a relic of St. Francis Xavier. When his coffin was opened, he was again found to be beautifully preserved: even his eyes were still completely intact. His skin had dried and tightened, but otherwise, the saint appeared lifelike. It was decided to separate his right arm and send it to Rome, since this was the arm St. Francis used to bless and baptize while he was a priest. That arm is still displayed today in a silver reliquary inside il Gesù, and, surprisingly, it is still preserved, although it has desiccated over the years and now appears to be mummified. All the same, the preservation of the arm after so many centuries is considered a wonder for those who honor St. Francis Xavier.

Another celebrated saint whose relics remain incorruptible is St. Catherine of Siena. St. Catherine was a fourteenth-century mystic who also actively worked to care for the sick during the plague years. She also visited prisoners, distributed alms, and actively worked to heal the schism that was vexing the Catholic Church at the time. She died young, at the age of thirty-three, on April 29, 1380, but at the time of her death, she was already considered a saint by numerous followers.

[38] Ibid., 149.

Because she died in Rome, St. Catherine was buried in the Church of Santa Maria sopra Minerva. Her body was exposed for three days after her death, during which time her limbs remained flexible, as if she were still alive.[39] A few years after her death, St. Catherine's tomb was opened in order to distribute relics to Siena, her hometown, where she had performed many miracles. Miraculously, her body was still preserved. The Church decided to give her head to Siena, and today it is displayed in Siena's Basilica of San Domenico and remains in a remarkable state of preservation.[40] Again, the skin has dried and shrunk, but you can still make out the features of the celebrated saint who is visited by thousands of pilgrims each year.

There are many more cases of incorruptible saints throughout the history of the Church. Author Joan Carroll Cruz counted 102 such cases in her monumental book, *The Incorruptibles*. As she wrote before the internet, she corresponded with shrines by post to confirm the existence and current states of the Incorruptibles she wrote about.[41] Still, nobody seems to have an exact list of all incorruptible saints. And as we saw with Sr. Wilhelmina, there may be even more Incorruptibles to be discovered.

The Incorruptibles still draw people to them. Some come because they are curious, and they find themselves transfixed by a rare post-mortem preservation of a human body, even if they believe that there is a natural explanation for it all. To the faithful, however, seeing an incorruptible saint is often part of a spiritual pilgrimage. For many Catholics, the Incorruptibles are a preview of our future and a reassurance that life continues after death. The Incorruptibles are also seen as

[39] Ibid., 92.

[40] George Ryan, "The Severed Holy Head of Saint Catherine of Siena," *UCatholic*, December 10, 2018, https://ucatholic.com/blog/the-severed-holy-head-of-saint-catherine-of-siena/.

[41] Cruz, *The Incorruptibles*, xvii.

witnesses to the holiness of the saints. Death is a consequence of sin, and the decay of the human body is a further consequence of sin. But in the case of the Incorruptibles, even the grave appears powerless, as these preserved saints seem to be so permeated with holiness that they are able to resist the normal course of death and decay. Pilgrims, therefore, flock to Incorruptibles to reflect on the promises of Christ and to pray for an urgent need. Some may have already had a devotion to the saint, as is often the case, but others may develop a devotion to the saint upon hearing the news of his or her incorruptibility.

I also think many people are drawn to the beauty of the Church's devotion to incorruptible saints. The reliquaries and tombs that keep the Incorruptibles are sublimely beautiful, and if you ever get to visit an incorruptible saint, you can't help but be struck by how much love there is for this saint before you. It is also moving to see around the saint's body or relics reminders of answered prayers and deep devotion. Such faith is as inspiring as it is beautiful.

Incorruptible saints are a consoling reminder of Christ's victory over death and the gift of everlasting life that He offers. That is why such saints are given beautiful tombs and reliquaries. These saints aren't a macabre attraction but an assurance that hope and miracles can still be found today.

Studying Incorruptibles

If you are unsure how you feel about Incorruptibles, even as a devout Catholic, you are not alone. The Catholic Church is reluctant to rule on Incorruptibles today, and incorruptibility is no longer accepted as one of the two miracles needed for canonization. The Vatican also conducts studies with scientists to better understand the phenomenon of bodily preservation and see whether anything miraculous is truly occurring.

One of the scientists who has studied the Incorruptibles extensively is Dr. Ezio Fulcheri, a pathologist at the University of Genoa who was first employed by the Catholic Church to assist in preserving the remains of Cardinal Josef Slipyj.[42] Cardinal Slipyj was the major archbishop of the Ukrainian Catholic Church when Soviet communists were oppressing and imprisoning many Catholics, and he served decades in the gulag before he was exiled to Rome, where he died in 1984. His life has been widely celebrated, and many believe he will someday be canonized. In order to conserve this holy man's legacy, Dr. Fulcheri worked to successfully preserve his remains, which were then transported back to his home diocese of Lviv in western Ukraine.

Dr. Fulcheri's work on the preservation of a celebrated Church figure made him the ideal candidate to become one of the many scientists the Vatican asked to study the Incorruptibles. Dr. Fulcheri examined several ancient and preserved bodies, both the knowingly preserved and those who were thought to be incorrupt. He, along with other scientists, spoke about his work and findings on Incorruptibles with science author Heather Pringle in her book *The Mummy Congress*, which details his first examination of an Incorruptible, St. Margaret of Cortona.

St. Margaret of Cortona was called "the Second Magdalene" by the bishop and spiritual writer Alban Goodier.[43] The Tuscan saint was born in the thirteenth century, a time of war and vicious politics, but she had been blessed with beautiful features, and men often tried to get her attention. St. Margaret eventually left her small town to be the mistress of a wealthy lord, and she lived a decadent and scandalous life.

After the murder of her lover, however, St. Margaret grew penitent, and she eventually went to Cortona to receive spiritual direction from the Franciscans. She nursed the sick women of the town and

[42] Heather Pringle, *The Mummy Congress: Science, Obsession, and the Everlasting Dead* (New York: Hyperion, 2002), loc. 2920 of 4577, Kindle.

[43] Alban Goodier, *Saints for Sinners* (Manchester, NH: Sophia Institute Press, 2007), 36.

lived a life of penance and prayer. Her last years were marked by great miracles, ecstasies, and spiritual visions, and people began coming from all over the countryside to see her for spiritual direction and miracles. By the time St. Margaret died, many people throughout Tuscany already considered her a saint. This feeling only intensified when her body appeared to be incorrupt, and many miracles occurred around her remains. For centuries, people made pilgrimages to St. Margaret's tomb to see her preserved remains and to ask for her intercession. Joan Carroll Cruz reports that her body was "light in color and dry but completely whole," with even her eyes intact.[44]

The Vatican had long wanted to study the phenomenon of incorruptibility, and so Dr. Fulcheri and a team assembled to research the remains of St. Margaret years after Cruz wrote her book. He and other researchers first took an oath with Church officials to respect the remains of St. Margaret and to report back the truth of their findings, then they began their examination of the saint's remains. Almost immediately, Dr. Fulcheri noticed signs of intentional mummification. Long incisions across her thighs and abdomen had been closed up with black thread. Several other signs showed that she was in fact an intentional mummy and not incorrupt.[45]

[44] Cruz, *The Incorruptibles*, 60.

[45] Pringle, *The Mummy Congress*, loc. 2973.

Whoever preserved St. Margaret had done so carefully and thoroughly. To Dr. Fulcheri, the procedure was reminiscent of Egyptian mummification, as St. Margaret's organs had been removed and resins had been applied to her skin.[46] This was far beyond the normal care given to the recently deceased. Then, to everyone's surprise, Dr. Fulcheri found records that confirmed that the preservation was intentional and even public, but this fact had been forgotten over time as news of the saint's preserved body became legendary.[47]

This is not to say, however, that all of the Incorruptibles can be explained as intentional mummifications or that the presence of Incorruptibles is an elaborate Church hoax. Some preservations can be explained by modern science, but that doesn't imply that all cases of incorruptibility are intentional forgeries. The body of St. Zita, for example, who died in 1278, was found incorrupt when her casket was opened two centuries later. Yet her body has been thoroughly examined and researched, and it has been found to be free from any artificial preservation attempts.[48] St. Zita's incorrupt remains can still be seen in Lucca, Italy, not far from St. Margaret of Cortona. She is not alone; the bodies of other saints like St. Anthony of Padua and Bl. Margaret of Savoy were also studied and found to be preserved without intervention.

Even in cases in which there is no attempt at mummification, we know it can still happen accidentally. As we discussed earlier, sometimes church crypts are just the perfect place for preservation to occur, especially when you combine such atmospheres with the tradition of anointing a body and wrapping it in linen. However, we still can't explain all of the Incorruptibles, many of whom were not always buried in such ideal conditions. And if environment alone could explain an incorruptible saint, we'd expect to find more preserved bodies in the same tombs.

46 Ibid., loc. 2983.
47 Ibid., loc. 2979.
48 Ibid., loc. 3043.

No doubt, more studies on other incorruptible saints will be done, and I hope we will learn much more about this phenomenon. And we should never be afraid to learn the truth, even when an Incorruptible turns out to be a mummy, because it's also possible that we don't find a natural explanation. In those latter cases, the bodies of the incorrupt saints will become all the more special.

Ultimately, those who are inspired by the saints will continue to find inspiration whether the saint is incorrupt or not. Incorruptibility is often treated as a mark of a holy and good life, but it is hardly the sole reason why people flock to the saints. Those who found inspiration and a patron saint in St. Margaret of Cortona will continue to do so, even if she isn't officially an Incorruptible.

And so the Incorruptibles remain a mysterious phenomenon that inspires believers and intrigues the skeptical. They are a reminder of death but also of the hope that death is not the end of our story. Elizabeth Harper, who has done extensive research and photography on the Incorruptibles, put it best: "They are somehow both a *memento mori* and the opposite of the anonymous grinning skull. We will all die, but maybe, if we're very good, we can linger in this world."[49] And for those of us who believe that the Incorruptibles are miraculous, their mysterious preservation speaks to a brighter future when all of us will be reunited with our Creator. We all must die, but death does not get the final say. As the saints show, the impact of a good life can continue long after a person has died, and the miraculous preservation of incorruptible saints is just one more miracle God has worked in the life of a good and holy person.

[49] Elizabeth Harper, "Photographing the Real Bodies of Incorrupt Saints," *All the Saints You Should Know*, August 14, 2015, https://www.allthesaintsyoushouldknow.com/blog2#/new-gallery.

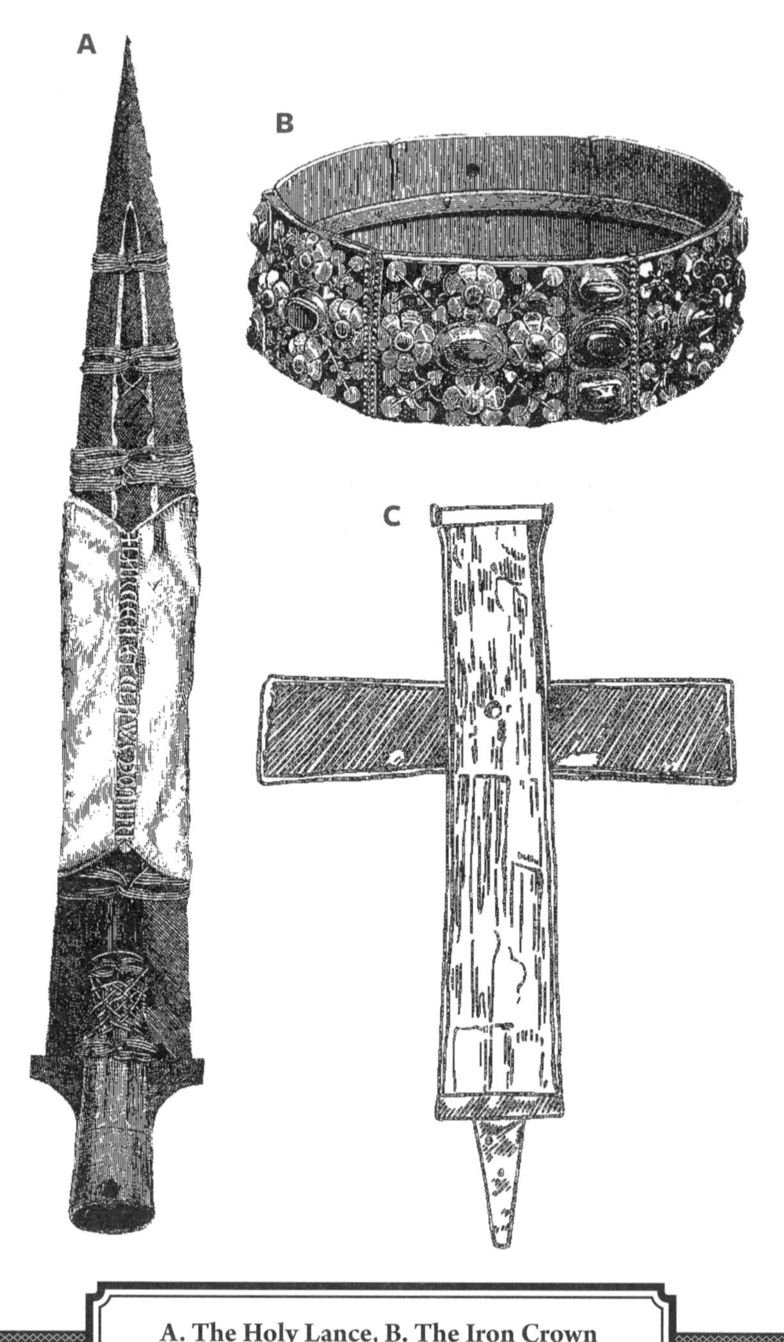

A. The Holy Lance, B. The Iron Crown
C. Particle of the True Cross

Chapter 4

The Weird and Wonderful World of Relics

HE INCORRUPTIBLES PRESENT arguably the most mysterious relics in Catholic history, but they are far from the only odd and miraculous relics. Relics play an important role in the history of Christianity, as Christians have been attributing miracles to them from the earliest period.

In some ways, the love of relics goes back to the Church's infancy. In St. Matthew's Gospel, we read that a woman suffering from hemorrhages touched the hem of Christ's robe and was healed. Jesus said directly to her, "Take heart, daughter; your faith has made you well" (Matt. 9:20–22). This garment had no power of its own; it was an ordinary object used by God to work a great miracle for a woman who had tremendous faith. Likewise, in the book of Acts, we read, "And God did extraordinary miracles by the hands of Paul, so that handkerchiefs or aprons were carried away from his body to the sick, and diseases left them and the evil spirits came out of them" (Acts 19:11–12). Again, these simple objects were powerless in and of themselves, but through the prayers of a saint, in this case St. Paul, they were blessed with the power to heal the faithful. This is effectively what relics of Christ and His followers are: ordinary objects God uses to work wondrous things.

In the early Church, there was especially a desire for relics of Christ's Crucifixion, and so today you can find such relics across the Christian world, such as the lance that pierced Christ's side and a Crucifixion nail, which are in Vienna's Imperial Treasury.[50] The Iron Crown of Lombardy likewise features another nail from the Crucifixion.[51] Such items would be used for coronation ceremonies and even carried into battle.

But outside of the pomp of royal ceremonies, relics are often in more humble places, like your local parish or in the library of a devout family. These relics are classified into three categories. First-class relics include both relics of the Crucifixion or of the life of Jesus, such as a splinter of the True Cross or rocks from Golgotha, and pieces of saints' bodies, such as bones or hair. Second-class relics are a saint's clothing, personal items, or other possessions they used often. Finally, third-class relics are items like prayer cards or rosaries that have touched first-class relics.

The faithful have sought first- and second-class relics since the beginning of Christianity, and that demand only increased as Christianity became more widespread. In most cases, relics were only distributed after the saint's body was reduced to bones, but sometimes, such as in the case of St. Francis Xavier, parts of saints' internal organs or flesh were divided for distribution. Such relics were labeled as *ex ossibus* (from the bones), *ex praecordis* (from the stomach or intestines), or *ex carne* (from the flesh).[52] Because there are more shrines and reliquaries than there are saints, many reliquaries today contain only small chips or parts of the body or small pieces of a saint's personal items. Yet these tiny relics are still the

[50] J. Charles Wall, *Relics from the Crucifixion: Where They Went and How They Got There* (Manchester, NH: Sophia Institute Press, 2015), 114.

[51] Ibid., 88.

[52] Cruz, *The Incorruptibles*, 149.

objects of great devotion. They are not just miraculous mementos but a way to connect with a saint and keep him or her physically and spiritually close. And if a saint is associated with a particular city or monastery, as we saw with St. Catherine of Siena, there is a special desire for his or her relics.

Some relics are so desired that they become the prizes of war. For example, King Baldwin I of Jerusalem was rewarded with a piece of the True Cross for his Siege of Sidon in 1110.[53] At other times, getting a relic was more of an adventure, such as in the romanticized tales of King Arthur and his knights seeking the Holy Grail. But sometimes the quest for relics has tempted people to turn to less savory means of acquiring them, and some relics have been obtained as spoils of violent wars or through acts of piracy and theft. These weird moments of history are what I like to call the Relic Fights.

One exceptionally messy relic fight involves the relics of St. Adalbert of Prague, a tenth-century Bohemian missionary and martyr. St. Adalbert was born to a noble family in Bohemia but decided to dedicate himself to the priesthood at an early age. Eventually, he became the bishop of Prague, but he was then exiled to Rome. Secular and episcopal politics prevented him from returning to Bohemia, but he still had a desire to serve the Church in whatever capacity he could. To that end, he undertook a series of missions, first to the Hungarians but eventually to the pagan Baltic Prussians. It was while he was among the Prussians that St. Adalbert was martyred on April 23, 997. His remains were ransomed from the pagans by King Bolesław I of Poland, and his relics were laid to rest in Gniezno Cathedral, where there is still an elaborate shrine to him. St. Adalbert

[53] Walls, *Relics*, 57.

was declared a martyr and saint a few years after his death, and that is when fight for his relics began.

St. Adalbert was a Bohemian man who, like so many prophets and saints, was not treated well in his homeland. However, after his canonization, there was a great desire to bring his relics back home. So in 1039, Duke Bretislav I of Bohemia raided Gniezno to steal the relics of St. Adalbert and bring them back to Bohemia. According to Czech sources, Bretislav managed to steal most of the relics, including the skull of St. Adalbert. But Polish sources say Bretislav stole the wrong head. So to this day, there are major shrines to the saint in both Prague and Gniezno.[54]

The raid on Gniezno is the most dramatic of the Relic Fights, but not the only case of relics being brought back as the prize of war. During the Crusades, especially the first three, faithful Christians brought many relics to western Europe after rescuing them from Muslim rulers or Muslim-occupied lands. Then, in the Fourth Crusade, Venetian soldiers raided the Christian city of Constantinople in an attempt to weaken the city and retaliate against previous injuries, and they brought back to Venice many items of religious or historical significance. However, the greatest prize for Venice is the relics in St. Mark's Basilica that were taken in a cunning adventure.

St. Mark the Apostle was among Christ's earliest followers, and his missionary work took him across the Mediterranean. He was martyred in Alexandria, Egypt, around 68 A.D., where his remains lay in a great shrine for centuries. But in 828, as Muslim rulers threatened Christian sites in Egypt, two Venetian merchants decided to take the relics of St. Mark with them back to

54 Masza Siltek, "The Threefold Movement of St. Adalbert's Head," *Mediaevistik* 29 (2016): 143–144.

Venice. They swapped the relics of St. Mark with other bones, possibly the bones of another saint, and then hid them in pork to get them past the Muslim guards. As the merchants sailed for home, they noticed that the relics would move whenever treacherous waters were near, thereby warning the sailors to change direction. When the relics arrived in Venice, the people threw a great celebration and held a religious procession to take the relics to their new home.[55] Eventually, Venice built one of the most striking churches in Christendom to hold the relics of St. Mark, the Basilica di San Marco.

Another example of force and cunning being used to acquire relics was when the relics of St. Nicholas were taken to Italy in 1087. We've covered the life of St. Nicholas and a few of his miracles, but even after his death, people were healed and delivered of suffering after being touched with his relics, and his bones still emit a miraculous myrrh.[56] And so when the saint's home of Myrna fell to the Seljuk Turks, several Italian cities vied for the relics of St. Nicholas, but men from Bari got to Myrna first. Once in Myrna, the men of Bari disguised themselves and made their way to the saint's basilica and tomb. Monks guarded the saint's tomb and so the men of Bari acted as pilgrims to gain entrance before revealing their true intentions. The men initially asked for the relics, proclaiming that they had orders from Rome to carry them back to Bari. The monks who guarded the tomb refused to part with the relics of St. Nicholas and warned the men that only

55 "The Relics of St Mark," The Fitzwilliam Museum, accessed March 29, 2024, https://fitzmuseum.cam.ac.uk/explore-our-collection/highlights/context/stories-and-histories/the-relics-of-st-mark.

56 Bret Thoman, OFS, "Discovering the Relics of Saint Nicholas … in Italy," *Aleteia*, December 06, 2021, https://aleteia.org/2021/12/06/discovering-the-relics-of-saint-nicholas-in-italy/.

God would allow the saint to depart. As the men from Bari got more aggressive in their negotiations with the monks, some of them drew swords, including a fellow named Matthew. As Matthew threatened one of the monks, seizing him and brandishing a sword, another monk begged the man from Bari to calm down. This monk told of a vision he and three other monks had wherein St. Nicholas appeared to them and said that his relics would be taken to a foreign land.

Matthew calmed down and sheathed his sword, convinced of the monk's words. He and other men got to work removing the holy relics from the tomb, and a priest hid them in his cloak. The men of Bari made haste to return to their boat while the monks began to cry out in agony. Through Providence, they made it back to their boat and set sail to Bari.[57]

After a long trek, the relics finally arrived in Bari on May 9, and miracles continued to occur around them. The people of Bari built a magnificent basilica for the relics of St. Nicholas, where they can still be seen today, especially on his feast day. The city and region also celebrate the Feast of the Translation of the Relics of St. Nicholas every year on May 9.

St. Augustine's relics also made it from north Africa to Italy, but this case didn't involve subterfuge or force. The Venerable Bede records that the relics of St. Augustine were first taken to Sardinia by Catholic bishops fleeing the Vandals. By the eighth century, Muslim soldiers had taken over the shores of Sardinia, and the relics were captured. Thankfully, the Lombard King

[57] "Medieval Sourcebook: The Translation of Saint Nicholas (Greek Anonymous Account, 13th Cent. MS)," trans. J. McGinley and H. Mursurillo, *Fordham University*, https://sourcebooks.fordham.edu/basis/nicholas-bari.asp.

Liutprand was able to ransom the relics in 724.[58] They were first brought to Genoa, where the king met the relics and brought them to his capital in Pavia. The relics remain in Pavia, just south of Milan, where they rest in a high altar at San Pietro in Ciel d'Oro. You can still see the bones of St. Augustine in Pavia on his feast day, August 28.

While disagreements about relics continue today, modern relic disputes are thankfully more political and rarely involve raiding armies or cunning trickery. However, these struggles are still emotional events that include ecclesiastical and legal fighting. We saw one such dispute recently play out over the relics of Ven. Fulton J. Sheen, a popular TV host and bishop whose shows reached millions. The beloved preacher was considered a saint in his lifetime, and the current cause for his canonization has attracted much attention. For years, Ven. Sheen's remains were interred in St. Patrick's Cathedral in New York City, but Sheen's home diocese in Peoria, Illinois, also sought his relics. Like in medieval times, it was a conflict between two cities that had a claim to a heroically holy man. Unlike past times, however, this case was simply handled in court, and the relics of Ven. Sheen were transferred to Peoria in 2019.[59]

The Relic Fights we've discussed are largely a thing of the past, but many Catholics still prize relics. For example, I am blessed to have a second-class relic of Ven. Fulton Sheen, a piece of his vestments labeled *ex vestimentis.* The relic sits in its small brass

58 Gregory Dipippo, "St Augustine and the Translation of His Relics," *New Liturgical Movement,* October 11, 2016, https://www.newliturgicalmovement.org/2016/10/st-augustine-and-translation-of-his.html.

59 Chris Kaergard, "Archbishop Fulton Sheen's Remains Return to Peoria," *Rockford Register Star,* June 27, 2019, https://www.rrstar.com/story/news/state/2019/06/27/archbishop-fulton-sheen-s-remains/4810794007/.

monstrance on a tiny shrine I made in the small room where I wrote this. Ven. Sheen died before I was born, and I never had a chance to meet him, but I still have a spiritual connection to him through his relic, which reminds me of Fulton Sheen's words, charity, and example. I'm also given the spiritual comfort of knowing that he is praying for me and my intentions. I can't imagine going to war for this relic, but of all that I own, it's my only possession that I would try to save from a fire.

You can find relics of all classes in your local parish and in the homes of the devout. Not all are as grand as the bones of an apostle, but they still play a large part in Catholic devotions. These relics are loved and used in prayers, processions, or blessings, and they show the faithful how the saints have a physical and spiritual presence everywhere. Every church altar houses a first-degree relic, and through these relics, saints pray with us through every Mass, Baptism, and other sacrament celebrated in each parish. And so, almost paradoxically, the saints remain in eternity while also being present in the daily lives of Christians, spiritually enriching the church and reminding us of the multitude of saints who will welcome us when we finally die.

Relics also speak to the Catholic view of death and the afterlife. They aren't just pious souvenirs but are indeed a real connection to the saints. Catholics believe that relics will join back together when Jesus calls all the dead to leave their graves. And until then, relics remind us that death does not signal the end of our life and work. Yes, relics are a reminder of death, but not necessarily in the same way as *memento mori*, for even when a relic comes from a body, its existence affirms the reality of eternal life after death and calls us to consider the legacy we will leave behind.

Finally, Catholics love relics because they allow us to see and pray with a saint in our local community. Not all of us can go on a pilgrimage to ancient Christian churches, but we can still visit an ancient saint in our home or parish. Every Catholic should speak with his parish pastor and ask which saint (or maybe saints) dwells in your church's altar. Consider researching that saint and his or her life — perhaps you will find in this saint a new patron or friend. Or if you ever happen to be in Pittsburgh, you can see the largest collection of relics outside the Vatican at St. Anthony's Chapel.[60] The saints who find a home in our humble shrines may be long dead, but they are still playing an active role in our lives, and their relics continue to remind us of the supernatural unity of the Church.

The Relics of St. Valentine

It's unlikely that the average person who celebrates St. Valentine's Day would think of martyrdom and relics. Despite its modern association with dinner dates and roses, though, the feast day does indeed celebrate an early Christian martyr whose relics are found in several churches. Some of these churches even hold events to see the saint's relics on his feast day, providing Catholic couples with a fitting but unusual St. Valentine's Day date.

Despite the great celebration of St. Valentine on his feast day, there is precious little we know about him. *The*

[60] Rachel Wilkinson, "A Pittsburgh Church Holds the Greatest Collection of Relics Outside of the Vatican," *Smithsonian Magazine*, July 2017, https://www.smithsonianmag.com/arts-culture/pittsburgh-church-greatest-collection-relics-outside-vatican-180963680/.

Golden Legend and other hagiographies record that he was a priest in Rome who was martyred by orders of the emperor around 269 A.D. His tomb and relics were preserved and honored, but as with so many other early Christian martyrs, St. Valentine's true deeds are known only to God. One of the more popular stories associated with him is that he performed the sacraments, including marriage, at a time when it was illegal to do so, which is why he is associated with romantic love, but he is also a patron saint of beekeepers and is one of the saints who is called upon against fainting.

If you go to Rome, tour guides will likely show you the Mouth of Truth (*La Bocca della Verità*), made famous by the film *Roman Holiday*, but few people go inside the Basilica of Santa Maria in Cosmedin that hosts it. Yet inside this basilica is a reliquary containing the floral-crowned relic of St. Valentine.[61] This ancient, Byzantine-inspired basilica is worth a visit by itself, but the skull of St. Valentine is the kind of wonderful relic you can find only in Rome. You can view the skull anytime the basilica is open, but it is customary to visit the relic on St. Valentine's feast day.

North of the Alps, in Prague's Basilica of Sts. Peter and Paul at Vyšehrad Castle, lies another relic of St. Valentine: his shoulder blade. While it is prominently displayed today, the relic was lost for centuries before it was rediscovered in 2002.[62] Nobody is

[61] Hannah Brockhaus, "The Rome Church Where You Can Venerate St. Valentine's Skull," *Catholic News Agency*, February 1, 2022, https://www.catholicnewsagency.com/news/246487/the-rome-church-where-you-can-venerate-st-valentines-skull.

[62] Raymond Johnston, "Prague Uncovered: This Neo-Gothic Basilica Houses a Relic from the Patron Saint of Love," *Expats_CZ*, February 14, 2020, https://www.expats.cz/czech-news/article/prague-uncovered-st-valentines-shoulder-was-lost-in-a-church-closet-for-a-century.

sure when the relic made its way to Prague, but it was likely brought to the basilica as a gift from Holy Roman Emperor Charles IV, who made Prague his capital and brought in many religious items. How it got lost is an even bigger mystery, but Prague and the basilica suffered through several wars, and there was also an extensive renovation of the basilica in the nineteenth century.

Further north and across the sea, you can find more relics of St. Valentine at his Dublin shrine inside Whitefriar Street Carmelite Church. The relics are contained in a reliquary beneath a statue of the saint, who is clad in the red vestments of martyrdom. Strangely, these relics were also lost for a time. They arrived in procession to the church in 1836 as a gift from Pope Gregory XVI to the church's parish priest, Fr. John Spratt.[63] The good priest loved relics, but they seemed to have been neglected after his death. They were in storage for a time until major renovations brought them back to prominence with a new statue.

While the relics of St. Valentine in both Prague and Dublin may have been briefly forgotten, they are now part of popular devotion. Many pilgrims stop by the Whitefriar Street Church, especially couples who want to pray for their relationship, and of course, February 14, the feast of St. Valentine, is a popular day to see the shrine and relics.

We here in the United States are also blessed with a significant relic of St. Valentine. Under the high altar at the Old St. Ferdinand Shrine in Florissant, Missouri, is a piece of St. Valentine's hip bone. This relic came to the now-closed missionary parish from Bishop Louis Valentine DuBourg, who received it as

[63] "Shrine of St. Valentine," *Whitefriar Street Church,* February 14, 2024, https://whitefriarstreetchurch.com/saint-valentine/.

a gift from the king of France.[64] The old parish is now a museum, but it is open for tours and rentals to anyone who wants to see a great glimpse into the lives of nineteenth-century Catholics on the frontier. The former shrine also hosts religious pilgrimages if you have the time to organize one and want to see the ancient saint.

Smaller relics of St. Valentine can be found around the world. They are not as well-known as the shrines we've discussed, but they still unite everyone who has ever sought St. Valentine's intercession. Like all relics, each relic of St. Valentine speaks to the eternal and universal nature of devotion to the saints that we see from our ancient forebears down to modern times. Highlighting these shrines shows us the weird and wonderful world of relics and how one ancient saint can be found in chapels and churches across the world. That a part of an early Roman martyr can be found as far away as Missouri is weird to consider, but it also speaks to the universal nature of the Catholic faith. Just as we did in days past, we honor the martyrs and ask for their assistance. The relics of St. Valentine and the shrines that keep them speak to the continuous story of faith, from the ancient martyrs to the living faithful today. Although we can get used to seeing these relics, I think it's worth considering just how odd it is to be able to say that we have parts of ancient saints all over the world.

It can be easy to forget these beautiful places of devotion, and even devout Catholics might not ever think to visit shrines and relics. But it is definitely worth getting to know the saints better

[64] Riverfront Times Staff, "St. Valentine's Remains Are in the Old St. Ferdinand Shrine in Missouri," *Riverfront Times*, February 13, 2022, https://www.riverfronttimes.com/stlouis/st-valentines-remains-are-in-the-old-st-ferdinand-shrine-in-missouri-photos/Slideshow/37395484.

through visiting and praying before their relics. It doesn't have to be an old saint like St. Valentine, as some incredible and holy people have lived in more recent years. But try to make time to visit and support them wherever you happen to be.

The Bejeweled body of St. Friedrich

Chapter 5

Catacomb Saints: The Bejeweled Skeletons of Catholicism

"And let no one, of things visible or invisible, envy me that I should attain to Jesus Christ. Let fire and the cross; let the crowds of wild beasts; let tearings, breakings, and dislocations of bones; let cutting off of members; let shatterings of the whole body; and let all the dreadful torments of the devil come upon me: only let me attain to Jesus Christ."

— St. Ignatius of Antioch, *The Epistle to the Romans*, ch. 5[65]

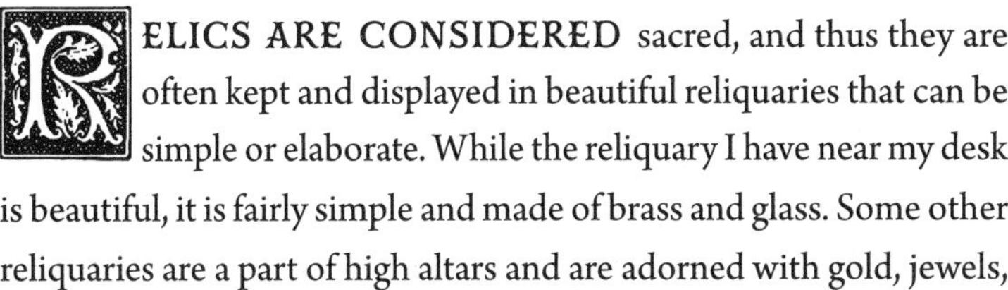

RELICS ARE CONSIDERED sacred, and thus they are often kept and displayed in beautiful reliquaries that can be simple or elaborate. While the reliquary I have near my desk is beautiful, it is fairly simple and made of brass and glass. Some other reliquaries are a part of high altars and are adorned with gold, jewels,

[65] "The Epistle of Ignatius to the Romans," trans. Alexander Roberts and James Donaldson, in *Ante-Nicene Fathers*, vol. 1, ed. Alexander Roberts, James Donaldson, and A. Cleveland Coxe (Buffalo, NY: Christian Literature Publishing Co., 1885); available at https://www.newadvent.org/fathers/0107.htm.

and precious stones that wow pilgrims. Relics always maintain their sacredness no matter how they are kept, but the beautiful reliquaries become works of art in themselves.

Sometimes relics themselves become part of the art. For example, in Rome's San Clemente Basilica, there is a stunning mosaic of the Triumph of the Holy Cross that incorporates several first-class relics. This twelfth-century mosaic is highly celebrated for its symbolism, which depicts the Cross and Tree of Life connected through a vine that also connects the Tree of Jesse, allegorically showing the whole of Biblical history leading to the Cross of Christ. At the bottom of this apse mosaic is a Latin statement that, roughly translated, says:

> We have likened the Church of Christ to this vine; the Law made it wither but the Cross made it bloom. In the body of Christ above this inscription rest wood from the Cross, a tooth of James, and Ignatius.[66]

That's right, they placed the relics themselves into the depiction of Christ in the mosaic. Having a piece of the True Cross in a depiction of the Cross is unexpected but also makes sense, but the mosaic also features the actual relics of two beloved martyrs. St. James was one of Christ's twelve apostles and had proclaimed Him until his martyrdom in the years after Christ's death. St. Ignatius of Antioch was another famous martyr who died in the second century. Tradition says that he was baptized by St. John and oversaw the Church in Antioch while also tending to the poor and destitute of his city. St. Ignatius was arrested during a time of persecution and was sent to

[66] Margaret Varnell Clark, *Walking through Rome* (Bloomington, IN: iUniverse, 2013), 87.

Rome in chains. There, he was sentenced to death and fed to wild animals before a cheering crowd in Rome, but now his relic helps to tell the story of his faith.

So there is a tradition of placing relics within art, but relics are only rarely used in such a way. During the Counter-Reformation period of the sixteenth and seventeenth centuries, however, Catholics north of the Alps practiced a new and unique way of displaying their sacred relics by decorating the bones themselves. These bejeweled saints are ancient martyrs who were rediscovered in the sixteenth century and given a new place in parishes mostly in German-speaking Catholic lands, where the Protestant Reformation had dealt great damage to relics and to their devotion.

These beautifully decorated bones are commonly known as "catacomb saints," or *katakombenheiligen* in German,[67] as that is their origin and is also nearly all we can say about them. Like the works of St. Valentine, the deeds of these saints are largely known only to God. Often, we only know a name and that each person was a martyr. Sometimes, we may not even know their names, and their relics are simply labeled *Incognito* or *Incognitus*.[68] Although we may not know much about these catacomb saints, their status as martyrs means that Catholics still see them as worthy of veneration. As they imitated Christ in their willingness to suffer death for love, they are especially viewed as holy models and heavenly intercessors. Ancient catacomb saints also stood as a testament to the long-lasting nature of the Catholic Faith, and thus there was a desire to send them north at a time when many in the Church fell under persecution or saw their friends and neighbors leaving the Church in droves.

[67] Paul Koudounaris, *Heavenly Bodies: Cult Treasures and Spectacular Saints from the Catacombs* (New York: Thames and Hudson, 2018), 14.

[68] Ibid., 54.

Thanks to the incredible work of researcher and photographer Dr. Paul Koudounaris in his book *Heavenly Bodies,* we can track the journey of some of these catacomb saints from Rome to parishes in northern Europe. When a newly discovered catacomb was searched for martyrs, these identified relics would be moved and made ready for transport. Then in Rome, under the care of the Sacred Congregation of Rites and Ceremonies, the bones would be wrapped in linens and placed in a wooden box.[69] That box would then be wrapped in waterproof cloths and wax seals.[70] Various groups and merchants, such the Swiss Guard, would transport the bones, and when they arrived at their new locale, they would be lavishly decorated by a monastery or parish as resources permitted. While some catacomb saints are hard to trace and might even be stored or forgotten, the ones that we can account for are often decorated with stunning jewels, fine clothing, and frequently a crown to symbolize their saintly victory.

I have had the joy of seeing several of these adorned relics. The most spectacular is the relic of St. Friedrich, whose skeletal remains lay in Melk Abbey, Austria. This abbey is a fine example of baroque and rococo art and architecture in general, but the relics of St. Friedrich truly stand out. His bones are arranged to appear in a reclining position, with his skull resting on the bones of his left arm. His skull is draped in a fine veil with a crown on top, and there are pearls where his teeth once were. The rest of his body is decorated with beautiful, embroidered clothes, and his bones are decorated with jewels.

Even though I make a habit of finding relics and saints wherever I go, I was not prepared to see St. Friedrich and his

[69] Ibid., 35.

[70] Ibid., 57.

stunning reliquary. At that point, I had already visited crypts, ossuaries, incorruptible saints, and several mummies. I was also familiar with *memento mori*. Still, I was taken aback by the grandeur of St. Friedrich's relics contrasted with the powerful reminder of death that comes from seeing a skull. I knew nothing at the time about catacomb saints, but I knew I had found another overlooked Catholic custom and a stark reminder of my own mortality.

Of course, seeing human bones is bound to make one think of death, and ancient bones often cause the mind to consider the passage of time. Yet the ornate adornment of jewelry and crowns is a bit of a preview of the glory that awaits these and other saints at the resurrection of the dead. The adorned bones are a symbol of the Church Triumphant, but we also remember that we can't experience that glory without first enduring life and death.

The catacomb saints also remind us of the mystery of the number of saints. We know the canonized saints, but we often forget that the actual number of those in Heaven is known only to God. Sometimes both the names and deeds of the early martyrs are a complete mystery to us. Seeing such saints in person often makes me think of how many other forgotten saints are in Heaven praying for us. So although I certainly think of death when I behold the catacomb saints, I often am also filled with joy in seeing such beauty around an unknown saint. The relics of St. Friedrich in Melk Abbey, for example, arrived at the abbey without a name, and the monks simply gave him one familiar to their own culture and time.[71] Now the remains of this anonymous martyr are venerated under that name in a stunning monastic church where they are admired by tourists while venerated by monks and pilgrims.

[71] Ibid., 153.

Venerating catacomb saints feels familiar to a Catholic, but richly decorating and displaying them can feel distant and alienating. Compared to other ways we remember death and everlasting life, even the odd ways we've discussed, these relics seem to be so much a product of their time and place. The catacomb saints documented by Dr. Koudounaris and other researchers are just a fraction of the hundreds of these martyrs who were once displayed all over the Catholic world, especially in German-speaking lands. But many disappeared either through neglect or as plundering armies picked out the gold and jewelry from their skeletal remains. Further, while Catholics continued their many ways of honoring and praying for the dead, some found the practice of catacomb saints just too much for the modern world. And so although catacomb saints continued to move from Rome to central Europe through the eighteenth century, they fell out of favor with more people as the years went on. The bones were often moved to a less ornate reliquary or sometimes forgotten entirely.

What furthered the neglect of catacomb saints was the lack of knowledge about these martyrs. As in the case of St. Friedrich in Melk Abbey, there might not even be proper documentation of the relics, which leads many to feel skeptical about the provenance of the bones. This skepticism about the catacomb saints and the influences of the Enlightenment, which sought undeniable proof and evidence of religious claims, led to parishes wanting to deemphasize the peculiar relics, and for some people, the lavish display of possibly unidentifiable bones felt like a superstition of a bygone era.

However, there is renewed interest in catacomb saints today, which means that the remaining ones may be present to pilgrims and researchers for a few more generations. Thanks to several books, the internet, and some attempts at preserving old Catholic devotions, the decorated bones are back to being admired and photographed.

Meanwhile, in the small Bavarian town of Roggenburg, old customs involving the catacomb saints are enacted on the feast of the Assumption of Mary, August 15. The Norbertine Abbey at Roggenburg is blessed with four catacomb saints, Sts. Laurentia, Severina, Valeria, and Venatius. As with the relics of other catacomb saints, the relics in Roggenburg were decorated in the nineteenth century with layers of robes, bodices, and veils, as well as papier-mâché masks over the skulls. These four saints are rarely displayed and certainly lack the jewelry of other catacomb saints, but on the feast of the Assumption, the monks celebrate a *Leiberfest,* in which they carry the bodies in glass reliquaries and take them in procession around the monastery and the village.[72] The procession includes a brass band, flowers, and banners, and after the procession, the brass band continues to play and food and beer are served, while the catacomb saints continue to be displayed and venerated in the monastic church of the Assumption.[73]

The Assumption Day festivities in Roggenburg offer a glimpse into the way our fellow Catholics worshipped in the past, and I'm glad the abbey continues the tradition. I have not yet been able to attend a *Leiberfest,* though it is on my list of local Catholic celebrations I want to experience around the world. Even without my participation, however, customs and traditions like *Leiberfest* are enriching to my faith simply because they give me an opportunity to participate in an age-old tradition. Such ceremonies remember and honor the martyrs and allow them to participate in the spiritual lives of the living faithful.

[72] Ibid., 16.

[73] "Roggenburg Leiberfest," *Atlas Obscura,* August 25, 2015, https://www.atlasobscura.com/places/roggenburg-leiberfest.

The fusion of devotion, death, and art that we find in catacomb saints is one reason why there is renewed interest in them and also why you can still find them across Europe. It's hard to compare them to anything else in the history of Catholic art and devotion, and it's especially difficult to find something similar that so vividly reminds us of death and the afterlife. But you can find these catacomb saints in places we've already explored in this part of the book, such as in the Capuchin Crypt in Brno, Czechia. As you step into the crypt, one of the first things you'll see is the relics of St. Clementiane, whose bones are fixed in wax in a reclining position. She is dressed in fine robes and has a wax mask over her skull, which, of course, is topped with a crown of victory. She came to the Brno Capuchins in the eighteenth century, but not much else is known about her, although it is believed she was a noblewoman.

St. Clementiane's relics are not as ornate as those of St. Friedrich in Melk, but they still provide us with a striking way to honor someone who died for her faith. Her relics are also the perfect thing to see when you first enter the Crypt, where they remind pilgrims of the ancient nature of Catholicism and the importance it places on honoring the dead, before you then notice the graves, coffins, and mummies beneath Brno's Holy Cross Church. All of these deceased Christians provide us with a sense of wonder that causes us to reflect upon our own mortality and legacy. And they absolutely raise the question of how much we desire union with God, especially as we consider our life after death.

The lavish display of the catacomb saints is not how most of us would want our remains to be honored, but the fashion in which their remains are venerated is still a beautiful way to remember martyrs as we also proclaim their victory in Christ. Although you might find them macabre at first, as I did, knowing more about their context and history reveals something familiar to a modern Catholic, as they are just one of the ways Catholics have honored saints and martyrs for millennia. And like so many of the ways Catholics remember, honor, and pray for the dead, catacomb saints remind us of how, even in death, we are still united to one another in our faith and our shared humanity.

The exhumed body of Pope Formosus on trial
Basilica of Saint John Lateran in Rome, Italy

Chapter 6

The Cadaver Synod: Putting a Corpse on Trial

UP TO THIS point, we've largely explored beautiful but unconventional ways that Catholics have remembered, prayed for, and honored the dead. While you might not be ready to bring a catacomb saint to your local parish, you certainly can see how these traditions are testaments to the great love and faith of our Catholic ancestors. Unfortunately, this love and respect is not the case with what historians now call the *Synodus Horrenda*, or the Cadaver Synod.

In 897, the corpse of Pope Formosus (r. 891–896) was exhumed and taken to the Basilica of St. John Lateran in Rome. This exhumation was not in the same spirit as the others we've discussed, but it was the start of one of the most infamous events in Church history. Pope Formosus, although he had been dead for a year, was being put on trial for a list of crimes. A deacon was chosen to speak for Formosus, while the reigning pontiff, Stephen VI, read the accusations against his deceased predecessor, which ranged from violating canon law by holding more than one ecclesiastical see, abusing papal power, and openly aspiring to papal power.

After hours of arguments, Pope Formosus was found guilty and was sentenced to have the three fingers he had used for consecrations amputated from his right hand while the rest of his body was to be placed in an anonymous grave. Later, the body of Formosus was thrown in the Tiber, and all ordinations by Formosus were declared null and had to be reconsecrated.

The Cadaver Synod was a gruesome and controversial event, both in the ninth century and still today. To understand these horrific acts, however, we should discuss the state of Europe at that time.

In the years before the trial of Pope Formosus, the deaths of two major historical figures contributed to the instability of Italy and other lands. The first was Pope St. Nicholas the Great, whose death in 867 ushered in a time of corruption and assassination in papal politics that featured at least two antipopes, nearly constant infighting, and as many as seven murdered popes in just over one hundred years. The other was Emperor Charles III, who died in 888. Charles III, also known as Charles the Fat, was the last legitimate descendent of Charlemagne, who had untied the Franks under one, great, Holy Roman Empire, and his death signaled the end of Charlemagne's great empire as hundreds of fiefdoms in western Europe fought for power and influence.

Along with the political and ecclesiastical chaos of the time, Italy and Europe were also under constant war and attacks. Sicily and other parts of southern Italy had fallen to Islamic rulers. Incursions were coming into Europe from Viking and Muslim armies, and even Rome was sacked by an Arab army in 846. Meanwhile, the armies of Christendom were fighting with one another for control and power, often leaving cities desolate and ruined. Particularly, the powerful Dukes of Spoleto were heavily involved in the politics, intrigue, and wars around Rome and the papacy as they aspired to gain the throne of the Kingdom of Italy.

Pope Formosus himself had been disciplined during his time as a bishop and papal envoy to the Bulgars by Pope John VIII

(r. 872–882), but he was then restored to his position by Pope Marinus (r. 882–884). However, the seeds for the Cadaver Synod had been planted. Formosus became pope in 891 and served for five tumultuous years. After his death, Boniface VI took the papal throne for only a couple of weeks before he died under mysterious circumstances. Likewise, just a few months after the Cadaver Synod, Boniface's successor, Pope Stephen VI, was imprisoned by rioters and strangled by a fellow prisoner.

The successors of Pope Stephen VI reversed the judgment of the Cadaver Synod within the year, and Pope Formosus was fished out of the Tiber and reburied in St. Peter's Basilica. However, the grotesque trial remained a controversial curiosity that inspired art, anti-papal arguments, and certainly a few jokes. For historians, the Cadaver Synod became the preeminent example of papal corruption in the early medieval period.

The horrifying events of the Cadaver Synod would be shocking to read about under any circumstance, but I think it especially stands out after we have explored some unusual Catholic burial customs. The many traditions we've explored may be strange at first glance, but we can quickly see how love and theology worked together to create something like a crypt or elaborate tomb. Christians consider the body a temple, made in the image and likeness of God, and it is worthy of love and respect even after death. That's why the intentional vandalization of a body is considered a desecration. But there is no respect for the dead in the ghastly deeds of Pope Stephen VI. Instead, the Cadaver Synod is more like the ancient practice of *damnatio memoriae* ("condemnation of memory"), when the memory of someone was intentionally wiped out of the history books and scratched out of carvings. The Cadaver Synod was an attempt to completely erase the memory and legacy of one pope.

Thankfully, the Cadaver Synod was a singular event, and nothing like it happens again in history. While there have been other instances of corrupt popes, none of them had the idea of digging up their predecessors for a trial. For me, the Cadaver Synod is the exception that proves the rule for how Catholics take care of the dead. A good Catholic always respects the body as something created by God, and that respect extends to the dead. Further, Catholics who die are still considered part of the Church and are still our brothers and sisters in Christ. We know that death may separate us, but we all wish to be reunited when Christ calls us from our tombs and our bodies and souls are one again. In the end, how we treat the dearly departed says a lot about how we feel about life, eternity, and the dignity of the human person.

Chapter 7

Remember Death and the Dead

E'VE DISCUSSED SOME incredible ways Catholics in the past have treated their dead and, the Cadaver Synod notwithstanding, how that treatment was spiritually rooted. However strange you might find these traditions, they are still beautiful works of faith handed down through generations.

You are not likely to construct an ossuary from bones found in your local parish cemetery, but there are many other ways that we can remember death and the dead. The examples we've gone over are stunning examples of *memento mori,* but they are not how most of us will remember our own deaths or pray for the dead. Instead, there are many holy and ancient traditions you can practice close at home. For example, the Catholic Church offers a plenary indulgence in November to anyone who visits a cemetery and prays for the dead there.[74] Some, like me, make this a regular habit throughout the year, but it's especially fitting to make such a local pilgrimage for the Commemoration of All the Faithful Departed, also known as All Souls' Day, on November 2.

Praying for the dead is an opportunity to remember the numerous people who came before us, especially the people who helped to

[74] Maura Roan McKeegan, "The Sanctity of a Cemetery: Remembering Souls Who Need Prayers," *Catholic Exchange,* October 25, 2018, https://catholicexchange.com/the-sanctity-of-a-cemetery-remembering-souls-who-need-prayers/.

build and preserve our local parish and community. As I've prayed for souls in a cemetery, I naturally find myself contemplating the universal nature of death and mortality as I confront the ways I will spend my remaining days. As Catholics, we also believe that praying for the dead is a way to find others who will pray for us. We intercede for souls and, when they are able, they can intercede for us. As the *Catechism of the Catholic Church* says, "Our prayer for [the dead] is capable not only of helping them but also of making their intercession for us effective" (958). We find friendship and purpose by helping one another and, as Catholics, we believe that continues through life and death.

You can also practice *memento mori* at home by making time to contemplate mortality and what that means for you. As I've mentioned already, books such as St. Robert Bellarmine's *The Art of Dying Well* and Sr. Theresa Aletheia Noble's *Memento Mori* are very helpful in teaching you how to practice *memento mori*. Each book has a different approach, as they are written centuries apart, but they both help to inspire devotion to this ancient Catholic meditation and will strengthen your faith as you reflect on life, death, and eternity.

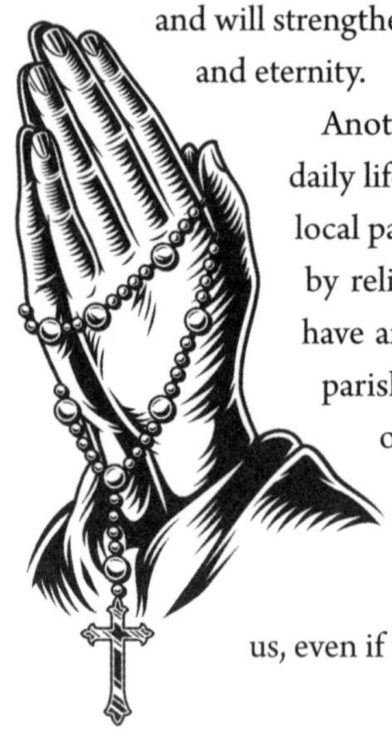

Another way to remember the dead in your daily life is to research the relics housed in your local parish churches. Our faith is strengthened by relics of all kinds, and while you may not have an incorruptible saint nearby, every local parish and most shrines are home to at least one relic. Relics are a beloved part of Catholic devotion, a connection between a saint and the living faithful, and we're blessed to have them near us, even if they aren't as famous or richly decorated as some of the relics we've covered. But you may start to look into your local parishes and realize that a relic of one of your favorite saints lies not too far away. Or perhaps you will discover a beloved shrine or chapel near you that, like a few places we've discussed, has been forgotten or overlooked.

However, I hope many of you are able at some point to find the time and ability to travel and visit some of the places we've highlighted in this section. If you do, you will find that it's hard not to ask questions about life, death, and our destiny in such spaces. I personally recommend going early to the more popular spots, such as the Capuchin Crypts of Rome and Brno, in order to avoid the tourists and crowds, but I also strongly recommend visiting some of the less popular sites, such as those listed in part five of this book. From my own experience, having an ossuary or burial crypt to yourself truly makes for some incredible times of meditation.

Even the devout Catholics among you may be unfamiliar or uncomfortable with some of the practices and devotions we've gone over in this section, and that is completely understandable, especially if you grew up in the United States like I did, where we don't often come into contact with the more ancient or medieval Catholic traditions. In addition, many of the places, devotions, and relics we've covered are also often depicted as macabre tourist attractions, which I think just adds to the discomfort.

When I first encountered an ossuary, I had no clue that these places would become part of my devotion and a bit of an obsession. While you might not become as enamored as I am, I hope at least you are now better prepared than I was to see and experience these things. And remember that while some of what we've discussed seems merely morbid at first glance, it all comes of a deep belief and hope in eternal life.

The purpose of this section was to show the great love Catholics have for saints and the dearly departed and to help us think on how we might reflect on our own mortality as we prepare ourselves for eternal life after death. The Church's love for the dead is driven by the belief that every human life is a unique and unrepeatable creation deserving of love and dignity. In ossuaries and crypts, we see human bodies as sacred art or tenderly preserved and prayed for across the centuries. Relics emphasize our belief in everlasting life. And although they have suffered neglect in the past, the renewed interest in ossuaries, crypts, and relics have kept these places and devotions alive and prove to the world the love the Church has for her beloved dead.

Part 3

Spiritual Warfare and Catholic Campfire Stories

"Since the devil and the demons wander throughout the whole world, and are everywhere present with wondrous speed, why should the martyrs, after shedding their blood, be imprisoned and unable to go forth?"

— St. Jerome[75]

"Modern people think the supernatural so improbable that they want to see it. I think it so probable that I leave it alone. Spirits are not worth all this fuss; I know that, for I am one myself."

— G. K. Chesterton[76]

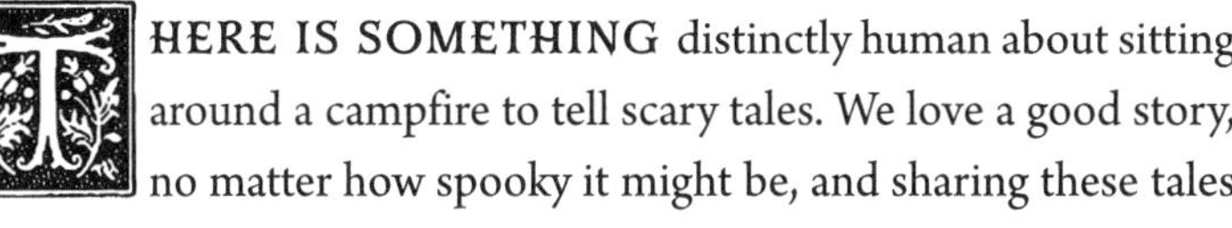

THERE IS SOMETHING distinctly human about sitting around a campfire to tell scary tales. We love a good story, no matter how spooky it might be, and sharing these tales with others helps to build community and friendship. Now, perhaps we don't sit around a campfire as much as we used to, and certainly less often than I'd like, but even in our technological age, we delight in hearing and telling stories just like our ancestors did.

75 Quoted in St. Thomas Aquinas, *Summa Theologica*, Supplement to the Third Part, q. 69, art. 3, trans. Fathers of the English Dominican Province (1920); available at https://www.newadvent.org/summa/5069.htm.

76 G. K. Chesterton, "Skepticism and Spiritualism," *The Society of G. K. Chesterton*, accessed May 2, 2024, https://www.chesterton.org/skepticism-and-spiritualism/.

Catholics have been telling tales of creepy things for generations. We read in part one of this book how many of the early saints were also exorcists who did battle with demons and, in a few cases, great monsters. Even some modern monsters, like the werewolf, are found in the illuminated manuscripts of medieval monks or in Catholic legends. Our Catholic ancestors also passed down stories of ghosts, purgatorial spirits, and heavenly saints visiting the living. These stories can be eerie at times, but many are also helpful and uplifting. And for many Catholics, both past and present, these stories are accepted as true. Some will even point to the physical evidence that these spirits are said to have left behind.

Some of the most famous and influential ghost stories were written from the Catholic perspective, such as *The Exorcist* by William Peter Blatty, who also wrote the screenplay for what is arguably the most frightening movie of all time. When *The Exorcist* hit movie theaters in 1973, it changed cinema forever, and it also influenced how Catholicism is portrayed in numerous horror flicks. Catholic themes also play a major role in the films from *The Conjuring* series, a successful cinematic franchise that follows a Catholic couple who investigates hauntings. These movies are also based on real events: Blatty based *The Exorcist* on reports of a real-life exorcism, and *The Conjuring* is based on the life of Ed and Lorraine Warren and their famous (and infamous) paranormal investigations. Fr. Gabriele Amorth, a famous exorcist we'll cover later, was not a fan of horror movies and often advised against seeing them, but he admitted that *The Exorcist* got some details right even as it exaggerated them, saying, "The film was made with much seriousness, but it is not without exaggeration: most of the time, the cases that exorcists treat are not as serious."[77]

There are good reasons why a Catholic priest wouldn't want people to see *The Exorcist* and *The Conjuring* films, and I'm certainly not recommending them for family movie night with the kids. Still, it is noteworthy how much the Catholic Faith has influenced modern horror. Even in literature, Bram Stoker and M. R. James, two of the best writers of spooky tales in the English language, featured a lot of Catholic themes and beliefs in their stories despite not belonging to the Church. And although most modern creepy tales may be fictional, much of their lore still has its roots in the stories Catholics passed down as true.

But the Catholic ghost story is also different from your average supernatural thriller because it affirms the Catholic Faith in all ways, including our view of the afterlife. There are tales of haunted houses in Catholic history, and some will remind you of modern stories, but they still fit within the Catholic Church's view of the Four Last Things: death, judgment, Heaven, and Hell. And while some would consider reports about purgatorial spirits and heavenly saints visiting the living to be simply ghost stories, the Catholic view of these things is much more profound.

The most popular and striking of Catholic spooky stories, and the ones that explain why Catholicism has so influenced the horror franchise, are those that concern demons. As we explored in the first section of this book, Christians have believed in demons from the time of the Gospels, and, at least in the United States, most Christians still believe in devils. About 57 percent of U.S. Catholics believe in ghosts and demons, and that number is

[77] Fr. Gabriele Amorth, *An Exorcist Explains the Demonic*, trans. Charlotte J. Fasi (Manchester, NH: Sophia Institute Press, 2016), 103.

slightly higher among Protestants.[78] This literal belief in the battle of good over evil is a perfect setting when crafting a fictional story or scary movie.

Demons are fallen angels who seek the ruin of God's creation, especially humanity, and they are the ultimate enemy in all Christian tales, past and present. Ancient Christian saints combatted these malevolent, inhuman spirits when they took possession of people or places, even though this often placed the saint in physical as well as spiritual danger from demonic forces. Even now, the Catholic Church still assigns exorcists to pray through ancient rituals to rid people of demons.

Are Catholics Afraid of Ghosts?

Catholic stories about ghosts, demons, and monsters are not always frightening. More often, the vexed Christians in these stories can triumph through God's grace and the intercession of His saints and angels. We saw this theme in the stories of St. Nicholas against demons, in which the inhuman spirits were terrified by the bishop. We can also see examples of when a Christian soul was at first frightened but was moved to pity, as in the story of the Werewolves of Ossory.

There are certainly tales of saints getting physically harmed by unseen forces, such as in the cases of Sts. Padre Pio and John Vianney. Even then, however, the saint resists the assaults of the devil and is victorious in the end. These tales are more extreme, as, usually, demons are just trying to trick or tempt their targets. Still, no matter how severe the attack might be, things that go bump in the night are thought of as ultimately powerless against God.

[78] Ballard, "About Half of Americans Believe Ghosts and Demons Exist."

In both story and doctrine, Catholics are taught that they can find courage and fortitude in their faith when facing ghosts or demons. We need not show fear while God is on our side, and we have access to sacramentals, saints, and prayers to strengthen our faith and turn away evil. However, it is natural to have some fear of the unknown, which is also why Catholics who believe in the supernatural will seek strength in their faith.

So Catholics are taught not to be afraid, but do they believe in ghosts? Before exploring the Church's doctrine, I think we should discuss the term "ghost" itself.

We get the term "ghost" from the German word *geist*, which means "spirit." The German term can be used to describe ghosts, like when we talk about a *poltergeist* ("noisy spirit"), but it can also be used in a secular way, like with the word *zeitgeist* ("the spirit of the age"). Of course, we regularly call the Third Person of the Trinity the Holy Ghost, a tradition we also get from English's German roots. We often use the word "ghost" to describe spirits of the dead who visit the living, but that doesn't feel like the right term when we talk about purgatorial spirits or saints from Heaven.

While St. Jerome affirmed that the souls of martyrs and other saints can visit the living, and St. Thomas Aquinas later used the words of St. Jerome to also say that the souls in Heaven can visit the living, no Catholic would call these visits from blessed souls a "haunting" because these visits are not meant to terrify or torture the living. On the contrary, visits from heavenly souls are thought of as a great blessing and a comfort. For example, Mary's apparitions are nearly always received with great joy, even if her message is a frightening one.

But what about the more malevolent ghosts? Does the Catholic Church teach that the damned can visit the living as they do in horror stories? St. Thomas answers that such a soul could visit the living but only with God's permission and "for man's instruction and intimidation."[79] Likewise, the souls in Purgatory can appear to the living through God's will. Purgatorial souls may be frightening, and God may intend them for instruction, but they are most often seeking prayers and supplications for their time in Purgatory.

One phenomenon we find among Catholic stories that truly frightens people is what Fr. Amorth and other exorcists call demonic infestation. Compared to possession, which is a demonic attack focusing on a person, demonic infestation is focused on homes, objects, or even animals. These are the classic haunted house situations, which Fr. Amorth notes can include things like unexplainable knocking, the sound of footsteps in empty rooms, mysterious voices or crying, and many other things you'd expect to find in a haunted house.[80] In the case of an infestation, demons seek to cause fear and distress for the occupants through these hauntings. In fact, the most common type of calls that exorcists get are about these mysterious phenomena associated with demonic infestation.[81]

The idea of a demon-infested house might evoke imagery from a haunted house thriller, but from the Catholic perspective, we are still not powerless against such entities. Through God's grace, the Church provides saints, prayers, and sacramentals that are powerful weapons against evil, and, if we need them, there are priests equipped to bless and exorcise a home. Thus, even in the most terrifying supernatural scenario, the Catholic Church has a storied tradition of the faithful's victory

[79] St. Thomas Aquinas, *Summa Theologica*, Suppl., q. 69, art. 3.

[80] Amorth, *An Exorcist Explains the Demonic*, 74.

[81] Fr. Gabriele Amorth, *Get Behind Me, Satan*, trans. Nicholas Reitzug (Manchester, NH: Sophia Institute Press, 2023), 21.

over the demonic. In the end, Catholics are assured of God's power over evil, even in the most terrifying true stories of the supernatural.

Bishop Germanus of Capua is visited by the ghost of the dead deacon Paschasius in the baths.

Chapter 1

Catholic Ghost Stories

N HIS SECTION of the *Summa* on whether departed souls can visit the living, St. Thomas Aquinas notes two saints who related such stories: St. Augustine and Pope St. Gregory the Great.[82] Both saints are regarded as Doctors of the Church in Catholicism, indicating their intellectual and spiritual influence on the Church; and both discussed the possibility of ghosts while sharing some early Christian stories of the dead visiting the living.

In a letter to St. Paulinus, St. Augustine discusses the appearance of St. Felix of Nola to the people of his city during a barbarian siege centuries after his martyrdom. Like today, St. Felix, known for his great care of the poor, was beloved by the people of Nola, so his presence during the siege would have been very comforting. This apparition was witnessed by several people, and St. Augustine wrote, "We have heard not by uncertain rumors, but by sure witnesses."[83]

St. Augustine is quick to point out that this event of a martyr visiting besieged people is rare in the order of things. The saint also notes that martyrs could only be "interested in affairs of the living"

82 See St. Thomas Aquinas, *Summa Theologica*, Suppl., q. 69, art. 3.

83 St. Augustine, *On the Care of the Dead*, in *Nicene and Post Nicene Fathers, First Series*, vol. 3, trans. H. Browne, ed. Phillip Schaff (Buffalo, NY: Christian Literature Publishing Co., 1887), no. 19; revised and edited for *New Advent* by Kevin Knight, available at https://www.newadvent.org/fathers/1316.htm.

through divine power.[84] While Augustine is correct that the appearance of saintly souls is a rare occurrence, there are other examples of times when saints showed themselves to the living during a violent siege. We already discussed one such event in the first chapter, when St. Michael appeared to St. Lorenzo Maiorano and others while they were attacked by invading barbarians. This story of course tells of a visiting angel and not of the soul of a deceased saint, but it is still part of a familiar pattern of locally beloved saints interceding during a crisis. Both Augustine and Aquinas tell us that such interventions are done to offer comfort to the living, so they aren't what we think of as ghost stories, despite their numinous nature.

St. Thomas Aquinas also refers to an account in the *Dialogues of St. Gregory the Great.* St. Gregory had his own supernatural experiences, and he had also seen an apparition of St. Michael the Archangel. The pontiff thus was a believer in miracles and listed many saints throughout his *Dialogues* who performed miracles, including St. Benedict, whom we'll discuss later. St. Gregory also tells of the souls of the dead visiting the living and recounts a chilling tale he heard in his youth about a deacon named Paschasius.

According to St. Gregory, by all accounts, Paschasius was a virtuous man. He was known for giving freely to the poor, living a holy life, and writing commentaries on the Holy Spirit. However, the deacon also got involved in contentious papal politics, and he was loyal to the archpriest and antipope Laurentius rather than Pope Symmachus in a short-lived Roman schism, during which Paschasius died.

Years later, Bishop Germanus of Capua made his way to the thermal baths at the recommendation of his doctor. As he entered the hot baths, Germanus spotted a servant whom he realized was the dead deacon Paschasius. Germanus was afraid at the sight of

[84] Ibid.

the deceased man, and he was also disturbed that such a holy soul was in this place. When Germanus asked the deacon why his soul was in the bathhouse, Paschasius responded that his support of the antipope against the successor of St. Peter was the reason for his time in Purgatory, and he begged the bishop to pray and say Masses for him. Germanus did as he was asked, and, after a few days, the ghost of Paschasius was no longer to be found in the baths.[85]

The account of St. Gregory's bathhouse ghost is a little more frightening than St. Augustine's story of St. Felix of Nola. In terms of spectacle, you can almost imagine Germanus seeing the shade of Paschasius slowly emerging from the steam of the baths. However, although it is a bit chilling, it is still different from our modern concept of a ghost story, since it remains hopeful and teaches the faithful that souls in Purgatory can gain spiritual aid from the living. St. Gregory's account of the ghost of Paschasius also follows some themes we'll see in later medieval ghost stories, which often feature purgatorial spirits reaching out to the living for prayers and other spiritual favors. These medieval accounts are still hopeful and comforting, and any fear in them quickly gives way to faith and hope in eternal life, but they will also begin to take the shape of what we would consider a ghost story.

Some of the most famous medieval, Catholic ghost stories were written around the year 1400 by an anonymous monk at Byland Abbey in North Yorkshire, England. These twelve ghost stories were written in the blank pages of a manuscript of theological works, and they preserve the oral folklore of the region.[86] They

[85] St. Gregory the Great, *Dialogues of Saint Gregory*, bk. 4, ch. 40, trans. Edmund Garratt (London: Phillip Lee Warner, 1911); available at https://www.tertullian.org/fathers/gregory_04_dialogues_book4.htm#C40.

[86] Eleanor Jackson, "Byland Abbey Ghost Stories: A Guide to Medieval Ghosts," *The British Library Medieval Manuscripts Blog*, October 29, 2020, https://blogs.bl.uk/digitisedmanuscripts/2020/10/byland-abbey-ghost-stories.html.

The specter of Robert of Boltby staring in the window to creep on the living

are local to Byland and therefore feature nearby places and people. The Byland accounts are also influential to modern ghost stories, as they were first transcribed by the medieval scholar and horror author M. R. James, who later used the Byland ghosts as inspiration for his celebrated short stories.

Most of the Byland ghost stories involve souls seeking absolution so that they may move on from Purgatory. As in St. Gregory's account, these spirits were often good people in life who had one great sin that kept them from attaining Paradise. Unlike St. Gregory's account, though, the Byland ghosts could be a frightening sight, and in a couple of stories, the ghosts become physically aggressive in their requests for spiritual help.

My favorite of the twelve Byland ghost stories is short but exciting. It tells of Robert of Boltby, who died young and, seemingly, with a heavy conscience. According to the anonymous monk, "He was accustomed to come forth from the grave in the night and disturb and frighten the peasants."[87] Dogs barked at Robert, and people avoided the dead man, but Robert would also frighten people by going up to windows and doors as if he were trying to listen to the living. The monk notes he may have been waiting for someone to command him to answer, in the name of the Trinity, why he was waiting around after death.

A group of young men decided they were having enough of being harassed by the specter of Robert, and so they made a plan to ambush the ghost one night. The rowdy youths made their way to the churchyard, ready to battle the ghost. When the ghastly face of Robert appeared, though, all but two of the boys fled. One of those last guys standing was another Robert, Robert Foxton, and his

[87] "Story III," *The Byland Abbey Ghost Stories Project of Saint Anselm College,* accessed May 18, 2024, https://www.anselm-classics.com/byland/story_3.html.

name is recorded because he seemed fearless. Foxton seized upon the dead man at the cemetery's entrance and dragged him to the steps of the church while yelling for his brave companion to go find a priest. Thankfully, the priest came quickly, and he commanded the ghost in the name of the Trinity and the virtue of Christ to confess why he was there. Robert, now yielding physically and spiritually, spoke as if his voice were coming from an empty jar and confessed his transgressions from life. The priest absolved Robert, and his ghost disappeared, never to bother the peasants again.

The longest of the Byland ghost stories tells of a tailor named Snowball (*Snawball* in Old English) who encounters a shapeshifting ghost several times. One of the shapes the ghost takes is that of a "figure of a man of great stature both fearful and lean, depicted to the likeness of one dead king,"[88] a direct reference to a famous bit of *memento mori* art that depicts three living kings across from three dead, skeletal kings.[89] After several adventures, the tailor learns that the ghost is the soul of an excommunicated man who requires absolution from a particular priest and who needs to have Masses said for him. After talking to several priests, the tailor obtains a writ of absolution, which he buries at the head of the ghost's grave. Thus pardoned, the ghost can move on to Heaven.

Compared to the accounts of Sts. Augustine and Gregory, the Byland ghost stories are more akin to folklore, but they too affirm the Catholic Church's teachings on caring and praying for the dead. The Byland ghosts are a bit more spooky, yet they still emphasize the

[88] "Story II," *The Byland Abbey Ghost Stories Project of Saint Anselm College*, accessed May 18, 2024, https://www.anselm-classics.com/byland/story_2.html.

[89] Sarah J. Biggs, "The Three Living and the Three Dead," *The British Library Medieval Manuscript Blog*, January 16, 2014, https://blogs.bl.uk/digitisedmanuscripts/2014/01/the-three-living-and-the-three-dead.html.

Catholic view of dying a good death and praying for the souls of the faithfully departed who dwell in Purgatory. A purgatorial soul may be frightening at first, but compassion and faith usually play a bigger role in these stories and visions.

But not every story of Catholics seeing spirits from Purgatory involves ghosts. Catholic mystics often have visions of Purgatory and of the dead who reside there. St. Catherine of Genoa, for example, whose incorrupt remains are displayed at her church in Genoa, had intense visions of Purgatory in the fifteenth century that she wrote down in a treatise. In St. Catherine of Genoa's visions, the purgatorial spirits experience intense pain and joy as they work through their sins. She notes, "The souls in Purgatory enjoy the greatest happiness and endure the greatest pain; the one does not hinder the other."[90] Her vision and the ghostly accounts we've read paint a clearer picture of Purgatory than how we often imagine it. The souls in Purgatory are still on a pilgrimage, where they experience great joy and sorrow, and they ask for our prayers as they seek to finish their journey.

Stories of purgatorial spirits or heavenly saints visiting the living are not just a thing of the ancient and medieval past. Of course, the tradition of telling ghost stories continues, but even modern saints have their strange accounts. St. John Bosco, one of the most beloved modern saints, had his own story of a departed soul visiting him one fateful night.

John Bosco came of age during the tumultuous early years of the nineteenth century in Italy. He was born in Piedmont a few decades before the Kingdom of Piedmont-Sardinia moved to unite the Italian peninsula into the Kingdom of Italy. As you can imagine, this massive

90 St. Catherine of Genoa, *Fire of Love: Understanding Purgatory*, trans. Charlotte Balfour and Helen Douglas Irvine (Manchester, NH: Sophia Institute Press, 1996), 68.

period of change brought a lot of war and other challenges to the population. John Bosco met these difficult times by establishing many charitable and mutual aid organizations to help the downtrodden, especially the poor and homeless youth, for whom he had great compassion.

Although he had a difficult boyhood, the young John Bosco excelled in school despite his troubles in paying for it. In 1835, at the age of twenty, John Bosco entered the seminary at Chieri along with his friend, Luigi Comollo. John Bosco would later reflect on Luigi and how much the young man had taught him about patience and spiritual life, and the two were close friends in their beginning years at seminary.

One day, after reading about the lives of the saints, John and Luigi were discussing death and wondered, half in jest, whether there would be any consolation in having a visit from a departed friend. The two had talked about this before, and so they made a casual agreement: "Whichever of us is the first to die will, if God permits it, bring back word of his salvation to his surviving companion."[91] It was a bit of fun between two promising young men, but neither realized the gravity of their agreement. Although Luigi was the more frail of the two, each thought they'd survive for many more years.

But Luigi Comollo died on April 2, 1839, just a few days before his twenty-second birthday. It's always sad when anyone loses their life at such a young age, but his death especially hit the young John Bosco hard. The next day, after the requiem Mass for Luigi ended, John Bosco sat in the seminary church waiting for a sign. He remembered the agreement they had made in jest, and now he was hoping Luigi would follow through. Unfortunately, no sign came to him in that church, and so John Bosco walked back to his dormitory in the pitch-black night.

[91] St. John Bosco, *Memoirs of the Oratory of St. Francis de Sales*, trans. Daniel Lyons, SDB (New Rochelle, NY: Don Bosco Publications, 2006), 98.

John Bosco was restless as he got into his bunk in the dormitory. He couldn't stop thinking about his departed friend and the wager they had made. In his heart, John wanted the consolation and comfort that would come from a visit from Luigi.

Around midnight, as he lay in bed, the young seminarian started to hear something. At first, the noise sounded like a heavy wagon being drawn by many horses. That was already strange, given the hour, but the noise kept getting louder. The noise was now coming from down the hall, and it kept increasing in intensity. Now the whole building was shaking, causing all the seminarians to leave their bunks and huddle together for comfort. John Bosco would later write, "It was the first time in my life I remember being afraid. The fear and terror were so bad that I fell ill and was at death's door."[92]

Suddenly, above the rumbling noise, all the seminarians heard the familiar voice of Luigi calling out three times, "Bosco, I am saved!" Not all understood the significance of this sentence. However, John Bosco and a few others who knew of the pact were stunned with gratitude by what they heard.

St. John Bosco would later recommend against entering into a pact like the one he and Luigi had made. As the saint later noted, God rarely takes heed of such agreements. However, in this instance, the mercy of God was such that John Bosco and several other witnesses were given a glimpse of the supernatural, and that gave them great comfort. The loss of his close friend and the ghostly visit had a profound effect on him, and John Bosco would later write a memoir about his friendship with Luigi. He himself would grow into a beloved saint and would soon be better known as Don Bosco as he helped countless destitute children in Turin, Italy, and across the

92 Ibid.

country. I do not doubt that he was also assisted by the fervent intervention of his dear friend, Luigi Comollo.

If you go to the town of Chieri, just outside of Turin, you can visit the grave of Luigi Comollo inside the seminary church of St. Phillip Neri. You also used to be able to visit a museum that featured the dorm where St. John Bosco and others heard the spirit of Luigi. Unfortunately, the Centro Visite Don Bosco museum has been closed for a few years, but I'm hoping it will reopen as interest in the saint increases.

The ghostly account of Luigi visiting St. John Bosco in the night has some mysterious and even frightening elements to it, especially the phantom noises and inexplicable shaking. For the people who experienced it, however, it was a moment of God's tremendous mercy when He allowed the dead to visit the living and inspire comfort and strength. Although the seminarians were first gripped in fear, their trembling gave way to joy when they finally understood what was happening. And so the account of St. John Bosco and his friend feels more miraculous than spine-chilling. There is certainly a feeling of fear in the story, but it is more like that fear of the awe-inspiring and otherworldly power of God. This fear is common when we glimpse the supernatural, which is why angels often tell us not to be afraid. So while the tale of St. John Bosco might make the hair on my arms stand up, for me, it is among the most beautiful and encouraging stories in the life of this inspiring saint.

We've explored a few examples of ghostly accounts throughout Catholic history, but there are certainly more. Some might be local to you. As we shall find, though, these chilling accounts aren't the only pieces of evidence we have for departed souls visiting the living.

The Museum of Purgatory

If you ever have the incredible chance to go to Rome, you are likely to visit the Vatican and Castel Sant'Angelo. For most visitors to Rome, they are must-see sites that are also sacred to Catholics. However, not far from these incredible places is another church that you might not even notice, the Chiesa di Sacro Cuore di Gesù in Prati (Church of the Sacred Heart of Jesus in Prati), a new church by Roman standards, built in the early twentieth century. Although a lovely neo-Gothic building, it would be unassuming were it not for the little museum at the back of the parish.

The collection in this one-room museum includes fingerprints burned into an old prayer book by the visiting spirit of a deceased woman. There is also a handprint left in some wood by a priest in Purgatory when his soul visited some nuns in Todi, Italy. This is the Museum of the Souls in Purgatory (*Museo delle anime del Purgatorio*).

There are countless museums and churches in Rome, more than you could see on a typical vacation. However, this tiny museum is worth visiting because of its unusual collection and its short distance from Castel Sant'Angelo. The small collection of about a dozen items isn't much, but it's the only museum I'm aware of where you can see physical evidence of purgatorial souls visiting the living.

The story of the Museum of the Souls in Purgatory begins on July 2, 1897, when a fire destroyed the previous church on the site of Sacro Cuore. As the parish priest, Fr. Victor Jouët, surveyed the damage, he discovered what he thought was a miraculous image: on one of the walls was the burnt-in shadowy effigy of a man with a mournful expression. Fr. Jouët thought this image might be a soul in Purgatory that was seeking absolution in the now-destroyed church.

Born in France, Fr. Jouët was a Missionary of the Sacred Heart who was devoted to praying for the souls in Purgatory. In the years before the fire, the priest had started an association whose mission was to pray for purgatorial souls, and he always remembered the dead in his prayers. Seeing this strange image in his destroyed church gave Fr. Jouët a new idea to collect evidence and documentation on visiting purgatorial souls. The result of this priest's collection is preserved in the present museum in the back of Sacro Cuore.

It seems almost miraculous that Fr. Jouët's collection survived his death in 1912. As we've seen from other cases, historical oddities like this tend to go into storage and become forgotten. Yet although it doesn't get the attention of other nearby sites, the Museum of the Souls in Purgatory has operated since the good priest's lifetime. It appears to be becoming better known among Catholic pilgrims, and I am hopeful that the museum will last for centuries.

While many other miracles and relics featured in this book have been thoroughly studied, I can't seem to find a scientific review of the museum's collection of purgatorial objects. I would certainly be curious for some formal study, but for now, the objects in the Museum of the Souls in Purgatory are still mysterious and strange enough to be worth seeing in person, even if you are understandably skeptical about these items and testimonies. I can speak from experience: the collection can affect people in the minutes it takes to see it.

The collection at the Museum of the Souls in Purgatory is made all the more striking after the tales of purgatorial souls we've explored, and it shows that there are certainly more stories of souls visiting the living. The museum also shows the Catholic approach to ghostly phenomena. Given that this collection is displayed in a Catholic parish in Rome, we see how the museum itself as well as

Catholic ghost stories in general serve to strengthen our faith and inspire compassion within us. If you view the museum's collection and are moved to pray for the souls in Purgatory, you are fulfilling a great part of Fr. Jouët's mission.

It's notable how much of what we've explored so far stresses the importance of having compassion for the dead. We have already seen in the rich heritage of burial practices for our departed Christians how Catholics are called to love the dead, and now we see how that compassion extends after death, as our stories remind us to remember and pray for the dead. Tales of the souls in Heaven visiting the living, such as in Sts. Augustine's and John Bosco's accounts, are hopeful and assure the faithful that Paradise awaits them if they practice the art of living well and dying a good death. These visits from heavenly souls also tend to comfort those who receive them.

The Catholic Church, of course, discourages seeking out departed souls. It's generally regarded as dangerous and opens a soul up to deception and ruin. However, through God's permission, the Church recognizes that there may be times when a departed soul appears to the living for good reason, such as for the instruction or comfort of a living person, as St. Thomas tells us. This all makes for some fascinating, hopeful, and even heartwarming ghost stories in the history of the Catholic Church. However, some stories from Catholic history are instructive in other ways.

Poltergeist from *The Wizard Clip* causing chaos in the Livingston kitchen

Chapter 2

The Wizard Clip: A Catholic Ghost Story in Appalachia

So far, this section has focused primarily on stories from Europe, but I've been hinting that some ghost stories from Catholic history are from closer to home. Our next tale takes place during the infancy of the United States Republic in what is now Middleway, West Virginia. This is the story of the Wizard Clip, a series of documented ghostly encounters that seem to blend Catholic tradition with Appalachian folklore. Numerous people witnessed this haunting, including an aristocratic priest who is now being considered for sainthood.

Servant of God Fr. Demetrius Augustine Gallitzin, locally called Prince Gallitzin or Fr. Augustine, is often nicknamed the Apostle to the Alleghenies on account of his missionary work. He was born into Russian nobility, but while on a trip to the United States in 1792, he gave up his title and wealth and entered the new St. Mary's Seminary in Baltimore, Maryland. He was among the first priests to be ordained in the new nation in 1795. As a multilingual and educated man, Fr. Gallitzin was ideal for serving the various Catholic communities across Pennsylvania and Virginia. To that end, he would travel hundreds of miles every week to minister to the needs of Catholics on the frontier of the new republic. He founded several towns, including Loretto, Pennsylvania, where he is buried.

Fr. Gallitzin's life and work have been celebrated since he died in 1840, and we could fill several books with details of his heroic life. Pope Benedict XVI opened the cause for his sainthood and granted him the title of Servant of God in 2005.[93] As well as being beloved by Catholics in the region, Fr. Gallitzin is one of several missionary preachers who have become part of the historical folklore in the area, with several parks named after him.

In 1797, Fr. Gallitzin was called to what was then Smithfield, Virginia (now Middleway, West Virginia), to investigate a haunting at the farm of Adam Livingston. The good priest had heard talk about the haunting, but he was not sure if he believed in it or not. According to a later letter, however, Fr. Gallitzin was "soon converted to full belief"[94] in the haunting after arriving at the farm, and he became a key eyewitness to the haunting of the Wizard Clip.

Aside from the letters of Fr. Gallitzin and a few others, most of the Wizard Clip story was passed down by oral tradition. It is the sort of ghost story that was told by the great-grandchildren of those who witnessed it, and as such, there are competing accounts and retellings of the haunting. The version I'll share is largely from Fr. Joseph M. Finotti's 1879 monograph, *The Mystery of the Wizard Clip,* in which the Italian missionary priest collected written accounts from Georgetown University and the McSherry family. The priest also corresponded with living witnesses, their children, and learned clergy. As a point of local pride, Fr.

93 Kathy Mellott, "Vatican Weighs Sainthood for Prince Gallitzin," *The Tribune-Democrat,* February 3, 2014, https://www.tribdem.com/news/local_news/vatican-weighs-sainthood-for-prince-gallitzin/article_c87e198e-ab05-5c52-bbc0-71d5316b67ce.html.

94 Thomas Heyden, *A Memoir on the Life and Character of Rev. Prince Demetrius A. de Gallitzin* (Baltimore: John Murphy and Co., 1869), 190.

Finotti was also the pastor of a parish I've frequently attended, St. Mary of the Assumption in Central City, Colorado. Additionally, I've used a more recent book, *The Appalachian Legend of the Wizard Clip,* a valuable work of research on the sources and stories behind this strange haunting, by author and local folklorist Michael Kishbucher.

Like many ghost stories, the Wizard Clip legend begins on a dark, rainy night inside an isolated house. Adam Livingston, his wife Mary, and their children were eating dinner around the fire when they jumped at the sound of three loud knocks on the door. Adam went to open the door, nervous about who could be knocking at this hour and during such a storm. He opened the door to find an unkempt stranger in wet clothes. The stranger spoke in an Irish accent and asked for shelter from the violent storm.

The Livingstons had a reputation for charity and hospitality, and so they got the stranger dry clothes and food, and the children set up a temporary bed for him. The stranger was grateful, but he was clearly exhausted from his journey and soon retired for the night. Later that evening, the stranger began to cough loudly enough to wake up Adam and the rest of the family. When Adam entered the room, he found the stranger sitting up on the bed, appearing to be at death's door. Knowing he had precious little time left, the stranger asked Adam to find him a priest.

The Livingston farm was about forty miles from the nearest priest, and it would be a dangerous journey in the ongoing storm. So Adam Livingston declined the stranger's request. Later sources also say that Adam, being a Lutheran, was also reluctant to invite a Roman Catholic priest into his home. Either way, Adam was not able or willing to fulfill the stranger's request, despite his pleadings. The stranger died just after midnight, and the haunting activity began soon after.

One account has that Adam employed a man named Jacob Foster to keep vigil with the dead man that night.[95] I'm unsure if Foster was a neighbor or the name of one of the Livingston's four slaves who are often absent from these accounts. Either way, Foster was unable to keep vigil, as the candles kept mysteriously blowing out. Adam tried lighting candles outside the room, which worked, but they would blow out the moment they came near the stranger's body. Jacob Foster left the house out of fear, refusing to keep vigil.

The next morning, Adam and Mary searched the stranger's items to try to identify him. He was nameless to his hosts, and none of his papers gave a hint to his identity. Without any other option, Adam buried the stranger in the unconsecrated ground on the family's property.

The next night, the noises began. At first, these noises sounded like galloping horses charging around the outside of the Livingston house. Several times, Adam was disturbed from his sleep and went to investigate the noise, but he found nothing that could explain it, even as he kept hearing the horses. Soon, it started to sound like the horses were coming from the walls.

The haunting activity kept increasing from there. The Livingston family was assaulted by poltergeist activity, even witnessing their furniture move seemingly on its own. Money and other items disappeared without a trace, and the phenomena seemed to intensify each night. Fr. Finotti sums up the intensifying haunting:

> His property was destroyed, his barn was burnt, his cattle all died, his clothes were cut all to pieces, his

[95] Michael Kishbucher, *The Appalachian Legend of the Wizard Clip* (Charleston, SC: The History Press, 2023), loc. 489 of 2555, Kindle.

> beds were burnt or cut.... The plates and all the crockery were thrown upon the floor.[96]

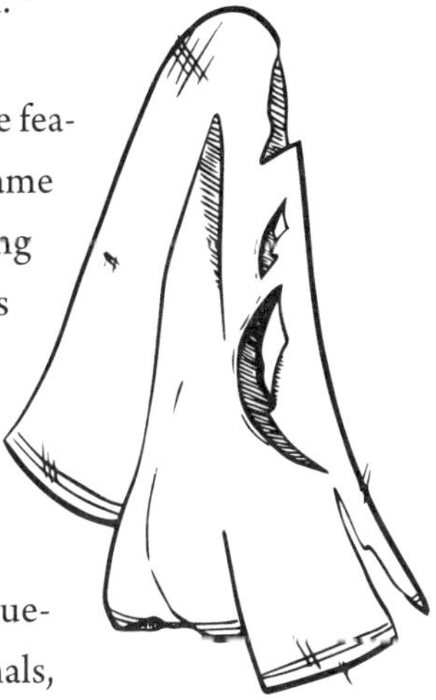

The cuttings are perhaps the most incredible feature of this tale. The Wizard Clip gets its name from the phantom sound of shears opening and shutting that the family and neighbors would often hear before finding crescent moon shapes cut into their clothing or household linens. Even items secured in pockets or trunks would get attacked by the invisible shears. However, the most gruesome was the Wizard Clip's attacks on animals, including an incident where it cleanly decapitated a flock of ducks. Some accounts say that the family couldn't keep any birds on the farm for fear of the Wizard Clip.[97]

Neighbors heard about the haunting and came to witness it themselves, including Adam's closest neighbors, the Irish Catholic McSherrys, who lived four miles away. Many of our primary sources come from the wife of this family, Anastasia McSherry, and her descendants.[98] They may have been the first to suggest finding a Catholic priest, but multiple accounts tell us that Adam tried first to contact his Lutheran pastor. Unfortunately, the Lutheran pastor did not believe he could exorcise the entity, so Adam next sought help from a Methodist and then an Episcopalian minister, both of whom were unable to deliver him from the haunting.

96 Rev. Joseph M. Finotti, *The Mystery of the Wizard Cip* (Baltimore: Kelly, Piet, and Company, 1879), 2.

97 Kishbucher, *The Appalachian Legend of the Wizard Clip,* loc. 822.

98 Ibid., loc. 554.

The haunting increased, with the spirit now moving even hot coals and burning logs to the point that the family was terrified to keep a fire, even on the coldest nights. Throughout the day, they also couldn't escape the noises, especially of that now-familiar clipping sound. Adam grew so desperate, he even consulted with folk magic conjurers to rid his land of the malevolent spirit. One conjurer gave Adam some herbs and other tools to cleanse his home, but they all were taken by the spirit and deposited into the chamber pot.

Some accounts tell us that Adam had a dream that gave him hope. In the dream, he saw an unfamiliar man wearing strange robes. As Adam looked at the man, he heard a voice proclaim, "This is the man who will bring you relief." Adam woke up and immediately tried to figure out who this unknown man could be. Perhaps he spoke with the McSherrys, who would have told him about the priest who said Mass in a nearby town. At any rate, when Adam attended Mass in Shepherdstown, he saw the face of Fr. Dennis Cahill and cried out, "The very man I saw in my dream!"[99]

After Mass, Adam approached Fr. Cahill and told him about the ghostly attacks. Fr. Cahill was a missionary priest from Ireland who visited parishes across the region each Sunday and was also familiar with the McSherrys. However, he didn't believe the stories Adam told him. The priest laughed and tried to reassure Adam that he was not being haunted and was likely the victim of a neighbor's prank. Adam was distraught and tried to convince the priest. Thankfully, several of Adam's neighbors, including Anastasia McSherry, were in attendance, and they also told the priest about the strange noises and cuttings they had witnessed. Hearing all this, Fr. Cahill reluctantly agreed to come and bless the house.

When Fr. Cahill came to the Livingston farm, the activity seemed to subside. The priest went around the house and blessed each room with holy water, reciting formal Latin prayers the whole

[99] Ibid., loc. 256.

time. Almost immediately, the missing money materialized on the floor. The family experienced peace for days after Fr. Cahill's blessing, but they called upon him again only two weeks later when the haunting activity resumed with the same intensity. Fr. Cahill decided that the family home needed an exorcism, and he called upon his fellow missionary priest, Fr. Augustine Gallitzin, to assist him.

Fr. Gallitzin lived with the Livingstons and the McSherrys for three months in 1797 to help Fr. Cahill with the investigation. During the first few days, Fr. Gallitzin interviewed all the witnesses he could find and recorded the accounts by hand. Unfortunately, the records were so widely read that they became lost.[100] All we have about this priest's experience is contained in a couple of his letters.

The two priests were able to exorcise the entity from the home, and Fr. Cahill instructed the family in the Catholic Faith. In a letter to the McSherry's daughter, Fr. Gallitzin records that the destructive activity halted once Mass was celebrated by Fr. Cahill in the Livingston home.[101] However, the family's experience with the supernatural continued.

Not long after the destructive activity ceased, the Livingstons were visited by another stranger. This stranger wore poor clothes and no shoes, but he declined a pair of shoes offered by Adam, saying that he didn't need shoes and was only there to instruct the family in the ways of his Father. The young man stayed with them for three days and instructed them in the basics of the Catholic Faith. After his visit, the young man walked into the field and disappeared. Adam would later say that an angel had visited them.[102]

After the family had attended multiple Masses, Adam was awakened one night by a bright light. To his surprise, a voice came from the light

100 Heyden, *A Memoir on the Life and Character of Rev. Prince Demetrius A. de Gallitzin,* 191.

101 Ibid., 193.

102 Kishbucher, *The Appalachian Legend of the Wizard Clip,* loc. 1165.

and instructed Adam not to be afraid. The Voice, as it is called, appeared frequently as a bright light and would instruct the family in all manner of Catholic things, such as the Eucharist and other sacraments. The Voice especially stressed the importance of praying for the dead.

The Voice would frequently wake the family to pray for three hours at a time. When the Livingstons would object to praying so much for the dead, the Voice began to emanate horrifying screams and pleas. The Voice said that these screams were coming from the souls in Purgatory who needed their prayers. The family was further convinced when a purgatorial handprint was burned onto a spare coat and towel the family had. This wasn't the only time the Voice burned things into items; once, it also burned IHS (an abbreviated form of the name of Jesus) into a goatskin vest.

According to some sources, the Voice said it was itself a purgatorial soul that was there to teach the family about the Catholic Faith and the importance of praying for the dead. Other times, the Voice would chastise the family for particular sins, such as vanity. The Voice continued to instruct the family for years, and it was even heard by other people, such as the McSherrys. According to Catholic sources, the Voice continued to appear to Adam Livingston until about 1814, shortly before his death.[103] By this time, Adam and the rest of the Livingstons had relocated to their home state of Pennsylvania, but it seems that the Voice followed them.

Before going back to Pennsylvania, Adam Livingston donated thirty-eight acres of his land to a Catholic trust in 1802. That land is still used today as a Catholic retreat center called Priest's Field. In this serene retreat center, you can find memorials to Adam Livingston, the stranger's grave, and other mementos from the mystery of the Wizard Clip. The town of Middleway also has historical markers to

[103] Ibid., loc. 1323.

show where the haunting was experienced. Those markers, of course, feature a pair of shears and a crescent moon.

Examining a Ghost Story

The Wizard Clip is a fascinating ghost story from the early days of the United States. While the haunting was witnessed by various people who wrote about their experiences, such as Fr. Gallitzin and the McSherry children, unfortunately, much of that witness testimony has been lost to time, and what we have today is largely preserved in family tradition and oral history from the region.

From a Catholic perspective, the Wizard Clip has a lot in common with other Catholic ghost stories we've explored. However, the first half of the Wizard Clip haunting sounds like Fr. Amorth's description of a demonic infestation, when demons seek to distress people through phenomena like strange noises, moving objects, and phantom voices. Given the malevolent nature of the entity, it certainly seems demonic. That the malevolence ceased after an exorcism and Mass speaks to the phenomenon being a demonic infestation. Fr. Amorth himself even notes that in his work as an exorcist, whenever he had to exorcise buildings, he often suggested saying Mass after the exorcism to fully remove the demonic infestation.

Although the legend is so steeped in Catholic tradition, it's hard to make a judgment of the story because of how much remains unknown. We have enough documentation to say that something happened to the Livingstons and their neighbors in the 1790s, but so many sources are from decades after the events or are lost entirely. As such, there are a lot of legends that get mixed up in the retelling of the Wizard Clip.

For example, in my retelling of the haunting, I mentioned the incident of the Irish stranger who showed up on that dark and stormy night and died in the Livingston's home. This stranger does not feature in Fr. Finotti's monograph, with one brief exception, nor does he appear in Fr. Gallitzin's surviving letters. Although he is now a popular part of the story, the stranger is not included in any written versions of the Wizard Clip until 1883.[104] Chances are, the mysterious, dying stranger is a later, Victorian-inspired tradition.

The dying stranger gives the ghost story a nice beginning, but there is some evidence that the hauntings began even earlier. According to the McSherry family tradition, the ghostly occurrences started in 1790, when the family still lived in Pennsylvania. The haunting merely followed them to Virginia.[105] Even with this family story, it's hard to find a source that gives an exact date for when the haunting began.

Finding where history ends and folktales begin is difficult to discern before we even discuss the Voice or the angel. The angel appears at different points in the story, depending on who is telling it. Similarly, the Voice is treated differently in Catholic and non-Catholic sources. For Catholics, the Voice is a helpful soul that was permitted by God to appear to the family from Purgatory to instruct them in the Faith. Although it can be demanding at times, the Voice's goals seemed to be aimed at the family's instruction in the Faith and to assist souls in Purgatory. The words and very existence of the Voice give proof to Catholic doctrine and hope in life after death.

In other retellings, the Voice is either glossed over or missing. Fr. Gallitzin only briefly mentions the Voice, and much of the post-exorcism tale comes from McSherry family lore.[106] For some modern readers, the Voice even comes across as slightly less terrifying but somehow still more annoying than a poltergeist. The Voice put a lot of demands on the family, insisting that they pray throughout the day and practice regular fasting, and it was quite insistent on avoiding all forms of vanity. The Voice also knew hidden things like when people

[104] Ibid., loc. 479.
[105] Ibid., loc. 756.
[106] Ibid., 1156.

were going to die or the state of souls in the afterlife, which adds to any discomfort a reader may feel.

The tale of the Wizard Clip is a story of supernatural terror at first, but it is also a conversion story. Fr. Finotti even titled his retelling "Livingston's Conversion." In the middle of the phantom shears, cut-up clothes, strange noises, and other hauntings, there is a story of how a Lutheran family became Catholic. So while the Wizard Clip is indeed an early Appalachian ghost story, it is also an account of a successful exorcism and a family's conversion to Catholicism.

As I've said a few times now, there are overlooked and wondrous bits of our Catholic history in the most unlikely of places, and some of them may be local to you. My initial interest in this story began because I learned about Fr. Finotti from a friend who shared my interest in Colorado history, and I quickly learned about his book on the Wizard Clip. Since then, my interest in these kinds of overlooked stories has only grown, and I hope that my retelling of this tale will inspire more people to explore this and other stories from our Catholic past.

For the sake of brevity, I haven't included all the details here about the Wizard Clip. The tale intersects with a few interesting figures in United States and Catholic history and local folklore. If you want to learn more about this peculiar haunting, I suggest reading the books I've mentioned, which will also teach you more about our American past and the culture of this area of West Virginia.

Catholics still believe in the supernatural, so these stories aren't merely curious folktales of long-ago beliefs. All the Catholic campfire stories we've discussed so far reflect matters of the Faith proclaimed by the Church and believed by the faithful today, including not only the doctrine of the existence of Purgatory, Heaven, and Hell, but also the possibilities of the dead visiting the living and the reality of demonic attacks.

Fr. Gabriele Amorth
Rome, Italy

Chapter 3

Fr. Amorth: The World's Most Famous Exorcist

"Never! I have never been afraid. Not even at the beginning! Never! I always say that it is the devil who is afraid of me."[107]

— Fr. Gabriele Amorth

EXORCISTS HAVE A long history within Christianity. Many Christians even point to Christ as the first exorcist. In the Gospels, we read about Jesus encountering a man possessed by demons. The possessed man was known to live among the tombs, where he would scream and injure himself with stones. Neither ropes nor chains could bind him, as he possessed the strength to break them. When Jesus saw the demoniac, He commanded, "Come out of the man, you unclean spirit!" (Mark 5:8). Jesus commanded the demons to reveal their name ("Legion") before using His divine power to send them into a herd of swine.

Jesus then gave the authority to cast out demons to His apostles (Mark 3:15), and Catholics believe that authority still

[107] Fr. Gabriele Amorth, *Father Amorth: My Battle against Satan*, trans. Charlotte J. Fasi (Manchester, NH: Sophia Institute Press, 2018), 39.

remains among the bishops, the successors of the apostles, who will typically appoint an exorcist. Saints throughout history have been exorcists, and we've discussed a few of them, and the Church still trains and appoints priests to be exorcists. These priests usually go to Rome to study with the International Association of Exorcists, an organization founded by six priests, including Fr. Gabriele Amorth, SSP, the most well-known exorcist in our lifetime.

As an exorcist in Rome, Fr. Amorth saw dozens of people a day who were suffering demonic disturbances. By his estimate, Fr. Amorth prayed tens of thousands of exorcisms for numerous people, whom he called his patients. He was often called "The Pope's Exorcist," which is also the title of the film inspired by his life and work (although the story in the film is entirely fictional). His decades of work as an exorcist in Rome would be enough to make him fascinating, but Fr. Amorth was also an engaging writer who penned hundreds of articles and dozens of books. Through this work, his interviews, and his life, Fr. Amorth gives us valuable insight into the life and ministry of a modern exorcist.

Gabriele Amorth was born on May 1, 1925, to a devout Catholic family in Modena, Italy. He later often said that his parents were "two saints"[108] who frequently attended Mass and prayed as a family. From the age of thirteen, young Gabriele considered becoming a priest, but he was unsure exactly what to do. At seventeen, Gabriele met Bl. Giacomo Alberione, the founder of the Society of St. Paul and several other Catholic institutions. Gabriele told Bl. Giacomo about his desire to become a priest but confessed he was considering other paths. Bl. Giacomo promised to say a Mass for

[108] Ibid., 8.

Gabriele, and after Mass, the blessed priest told the young man, "You will join the order of St. Paul."[109]

Also at seventeen, Gabriele met another priest who would become his spiritual mentor, St. Pio of Pietrelcina, popularly known as Padre Pio. An influential priest, mystic, and confessor, Padre Pio often had profound insights into people's lives, and so Gabriele wanted to hear his opinions. He did not get a direct answer from the charismatic priest, but Padre Pio remained his spiritual director for twenty-six years.

The young Gabriele decided he would join the Paulines after high school. Unfortunately, the Second World War had begun, and young men were being compelled to fight for the fascist Italian Army. The future priest initially went to university to avoid the war, but he was soon drafted into the army. But Gabriele followed his conscience and abandoned the army to fight with the resistance movement in the mountains and plains around Modena. And so before he became an exorcist and spiritually battled demons, Gabriele Amorth was fighting physical battles with the same courage. He even won a medal for his valor. After the war, Gabriele entered politics. He became a leader in the Young Christian Democrats and served as a deputy to a future prime minister.[110]

Although it appeared that he had a future in Italian politics, Gabriele never forgot his conversation with Bl. Giacomo Alberione about becoming a priest. And so he resigned from politics, finished his degree, and joined the Paulines. After his formation and theological education, Fr. Amorth was ordained on January 24, 1954.

Fr. Amorth had a great love of Mary, and he was especially devoted to her Immaculate Heart. Fr. Amorth was born during the

[109] Ibid.

[110] Ibid., 9.

Month of Mary, and he was ordained during a Marian year, as 1954 celebrated the one hundredth anniversary of the proclamation of the dogma of the Immaculate Conception. After a journey to Fatima, he dedicated himself to the consecration of Italy to the Immaculate Heart of Mary in order to fulfill our Lady's request at Fatima that all nations be consecrated to her Immaculate Heart to save souls and bring about peace. Fr. Amorth set himself to this task and, thankfully, the bishops agreed to consecrate Italy to Mary's Immaculate Heart in 1959. That same year, he arranged for a statue of Our Lady of Fatima to be carried by helicopter to all the provincial capitals in Italy. Later, Fr. Amorth noted that this mission had been "the most beautiful adventure" of his life.[111]

Fr. Amorth also worked in many roles as a priest. He was a teacher at times and was also a writer and editor for several Catholic newspapers. He even eventually wrote a book about Mary. This talent for writing and working with the media would serve him well in his later ministry. Then, in 1986, after years of hard work as a priest, Fr. Amorth received a strange call.

At the time, there were only a few exorcists in Italy, and Rome's sole exorcist, Fr. Candido Amantini, was now advanced in years and suffering health concerns. For decades, Fr. Amantini had exorcized patients at the Scala Sancta sanctuary, and his superiors were now looking for an assistant for him. The Vicar General at the time, Cardinal Ugo Poletti, asked Fr. Amorth if he would be interested.

Initially, Fr. Amorth declined because he regarded himself as "a good-for-nothing, good only for telling jokes and playing pranks."[112] However, he eventually agreed to the new ministry, placing himself

[111] Ibid., 11.
[112] Ibid., 15.

under the protection of Mary. Under Fr. Amantini's tutelage, Fr. Amorth learned how to be an exorcist, and he would serve in that role until his death in 2016.

After assisting Fr. Amantini with numerous exorcisms, Fr. Amorth was assigned his first solo exorcism. In this case, the patient was a young, rural, farm worker who had reportedly levitated, spoke in languages he didn't know, and demonstrated unnatural strength. A few people were with the patient to hold him down, and a translator was also present, as the demon often communicated in English, a language the priest didn't speak. As Fr. Amorth prayed the exorcism, he got to the part where he commanded the evil spirit to reveal its name, saying *Praecipio tibi* ("I command you"), when the demon spoke through the young man and yelled, "I am Lucifer!"[113] The priest did not need a translation. He knew he was now face-to-face with the devil himself.

The room became cold, and ice crystals formed on the windows and walls. The patient shrieked and contorted his head and body. Fr. Amorth knew he had to continue the exorcism, although he was struck by the name. The demon announced that it would leave the patient on June 21, which was months away. After numerous sessions and many prayers, the patient was finally liberated on the promised day, but Fr. Amorth prayed several more exorcisms to be safe.

Fr. Amorth's first solo mission was intense and full of strange phenomena. He would face Lucifer again in other exorcisms, but he only saw a bed levitating one other time. Thankfully, Fr. Amorth found that horror movies had greatly exaggerated the spooky phenomena an exorcist encounters. He saw and experienced many strange things over the course of his career, but few of his

[113] Ibid., 38.

patients showed as dramatic supernatural signs as that first young man. But Fr. Amorth often kept a handkerchief on him, as patients would often spit during the exorcism, and sometimes he was spat at with nails or glass. In one case, a young man materialized three nails in his mouth that were then projected at the priest. Fr. Amorth kept those nails in his room and would even show them to journalists.[114]

As with many exorcists, Fr. Amorth found that cases of "valid and true" possession were quite rare.[115] Other types of demonic attacks, which we'll go over below, are far more common. While Fr. Amorth did experience some strange phenomena in his work, something that stands out to most readers is how the priest treats exorcism like any other ministry. As a writer, he knows when to be solemn and serious, but his sense of humor is sprinkled throughout his work. Fr. Amorth also showed a lot of compassion for the patients and families that called upon him, and he always consulted with doctors, psychiatrists, bishops, and other priests to ensure that the patients he saw received healing for physical and spiritual maladies.

If someone came to Fr. Amorth with signs of demonic possession, and if all medical explanations were ruled out, he would pray a "diagnostic exorcism" to see how the patient reacted.[116] Some priests have a charism for discernment, like Fr. Candido Amantini, and can discern the presence of demons, but Fr. Amorth said he didn't have such a charism, and so he closely observed the reaction of patients to prayers, holy objects, or sacred spaces.

114 Ibid., 23.

115 Amorth, *An Exorcist Explains the Demonic*, 66.

116 Fr. Gabriele Amorth, *The Devil Is Afraid of Me*, trans. Charlotte J. Fasi (Manchester, NH: Sophia Institute Press, 2019), 18.

According to Fr. Amorth, a more common sign of possession is the patient knowing hidden things. Sometimes, the patient would begin speaking in languages he or she never spoke before, or perhaps the patient had sudden knowledge of distant or buried objects. In one case experienced by Fr. Amantini, the demon said its form was buried in a wooden box. The demon said this box was three yards deep beneath a particular tree. Fr. Amantini searched where the patient had directed him, found a box buried in the exact spot, and destroyed the profane figure he found within it.[117] Yet while some people are afraid seeing an exorcism because they fear that the demon may reveal their private sins, this never happened in Fr. Amorth's experience.[118]

Throughout all these strange happenings, Fr. Amorth says he was never afraid. He was a long-devoted son of Mary, and he felt her protection. As the priest said in an interview, "I have my guardian angel; I have St. Gabriel, who is my patron; and I have the mantle of Our Lady! I feel like a lord; I always feel secure!"[119] Even in exorcisms, the demons would often cry out, "We can do nothing to you because you are too protected!"[120] Fr. Amorth also often felt the protection of his old spiritual director, Padre Pio. In a couple of the exorcisms he prayed, the demons would acknowledge the spirit of Padre Pio assisting with his prayers, yelling out, "Away with that priest. I do not want him!" In other exorcisms, he also felt the spiritual assistance of his deceased mentor, Fr. Candido Amantini.[121]

[117] Amorth, *An Exorcist Explains the Demonic*, 104.

[118] Amorth, *The Devil Is Afraid of Me*, 111.

[119] Amorth, *My Battle against Satan*, 39.

[120] Amorth, *The Devil Is Afraid of Me*, 39.

[121] Amorth, *My Battle against Satan*, 25.

Many of Fr. Amorth's patients and their families regarded him as a war hero in the battle against evil. One of his patients, after she had been liberated from demonic possession, reflected on how Fr. Amorth was like a brave and saintly warrior, saying:

> I clearly recall one thing: when he did the exorcism, he was like a war machine. He would go from the beginning to the end totally focused on what he was doing. Perhaps it is a childish comparison, but he seemed to me like a knight in shining armor. He would unsheathe his sword, and he would fight. He was not afraid, or at least this was my impression.[122]

People also remembered his sense of humor and warm compassion before and after an exorcism. This mix of solemnity and humor made him beloved in his ministry, and it also made him an intriguing figure for journalists.

Fr. Amorth talked about his life and ministry in his books, articles, and radio sermons, which brought him into contact with Catholic and secular journalists. Fr. Amorth spoke plainly and candidly about his ministry in interviews, and he was also not afraid of sharing his sometimes controversial opinions. The old exorcist spoke about spiritual warfare, demons, and the occult, of course, but he also spoke about topics ranging from ecclesiastical politics and history to yoga and Harry Potter. He felt that Satan was doing his evil work throughout the world, even within the Vatican. In Fr. Amorth's view, nobody was immune from Satan's false promises, and that included spiritual and political leaders. "Today," said Fr. Amorth,

[122] Ibid., 178.

"Satan is trying more than ever to lead as many souls as possible to an eternal death."[123]

Yet despite his personal opinions, most of what Fr. Amorth did for the Church was incredibly communal and inspiring. In particular, as he waged war against the evil one, Fr. Amorth knew the Church would need more exorcists. When Fr. Amorth had started his ministry, Fr. Candido Amantini was the sole exorcist in Rome and one of only a handful in Italy. And so, in order to help train and support priests in this extraordinary ministry, Fr. Amorth and five other priests created the International Association of Exorcists. By the end of his life, Fr. Amorth had trained and befriended dozens of priests, and he helped the number of exorcists to increase. Many of the priests who trained with Fr. Amorth are still active as exorcists today.

Even as his physical health began to fail, Fr. Amorth saw dozens of patients daily while making time for his books and interviews. In 2009, at the age of eighty-four, Fr. Amorth's health had declined to the point that he finally had to step back from full-time ministry. Still, he continued to perform exorcisms and assisted priests with particularly difficult cases. He also continued to speak publicly about his life and work. Then, on September 16, 2016, Fr. Gabriele Amorth died at the age of ninety-one. He left behind an incredible and ongoing legacy that will continue for years to come.

There are a lot of colorful and over-the-top characters in Catholic history, yet Fr. Gabriele Amorth still stands out. Along with his tireless work as a priest and exorcist, Fr. Amorth offered an open and candid look into the life of a Catholic exorcist working today. Even those who were skeptical or who disagreed with him found Fr. Amorth an intriguing and challenging figure in recent Catholic history.

[123] Ibid., 17.

Types of Demonic Attack

St. Peter instructs the faithful always to "Be sober, be watchful. Your adversary the devil prowls around like a roaring lion, seeking someone to devour" (1 Pet. 5:8). This verse is one that many exorcists refer to, especially when trying to warn people of demonic attacks. In the life of Fr. Amorth, it seems especially relevant.

In his writings and many interviews, Fr. Gabriele Amorth discussed a range of topics about spiritual warfare. Often, journalists wanted to hear the exciting stories he might have, but the good priest also spoke about the ways demons seek the ruin of souls. In Fr. Amorth's view, there were two types of demonic attack, ordinary and extraordinary.

The ordinary actions of the demonic are also the most common: tempting people to sin. "The devil's mission in the world," according to Fr. Amorth, "is to seduce souls, to lead each man and woman on the wayward paths of sin; and the principal path of this tragic mission is the path of temptation."[124] Temptation is how the vast majority of people will experience demonic attacks. Satan even tempted Christ in the desert. But Fr. Amorth found demonic attacks to be monotonous. The exorcist even asked a demon during an exorcism about the devil's repetitive behavior:

> We do well to remember that the devil is tremendously monotonous in his temptations and when I asked him about this, he confirmed this trait of his monotony, but also added that despite this, we men always fall into his traps.[125]

In some circumstances, though, demons may attack people through extraordinary diabolical action. In Fr. Amorth's experience, these extraordinary attacks include possession and infestation, which we've briefly discussed, but they also include vexation, obsession, physical disturbances, and dependency. Let's explore these six types of demonic attacks and Fr. Amorth's insights.

[124] Amorth, *An Exorcist Explains the Demonic*, 63.

[125] Amorth, *Get Behind Me, Satan*, 10.

Demonic possession is the most dramatic and rarest type of diabolical attack. "Without a doubt, diabolical possession, the invincible influence of the devil on a person, is the most striking and serious form of the extraordinary action of the devil,"[126] says Fr. Amorth. In the cases of possession, the demon takes control of the patient's actions and words and manifests through phenomena surrounding the person. The diabolical activity is not constant or permanent, but it tends to manifest when there is spiritual pressure, like during an exorcism.

Although he knew possession was real, Fr. Amorth also cautioned that such incredible and obvious signs of the devil are not preferred by demons. As such, a demon may try to hide or conceal itself from an exorcist, which is why Fr. Amorth always carried out an investigation and allowed for a time of discernment before he would continue any exorcism. In the end, a demon "prefers by far to act through temptation"[127] rather than expose itself in such a spectacular way.

Diabolical vexation is described by Fr. Amorth as "when the demon causes a person serious disturbances but not possession."[128] This can include attacks on the patient's body, relationships, or even their business. Fr. Amorth notes that vexation is often "caused by a person's cultivation of imprudent habits; by frequenting wizards or séances, through repeated and persistent serious sins, or by submitting to spells."[129] However, a few saints have also experienced vexation, with Fr. Amorth pointing to Padre Pio and St. John Vianney as examples.[130] Padre Pio was attacked by a demonic black dog in

[126] Amorth, *An Exorcist Explains the Demonic*, 66.

[127] Ibid., 68.

[128] Amorth, *The Devil Is Afraid of Me*, 112.

[129] Amorth, *An Exorcist Explains the Demonic*, 70.

[130] Ibid., 72.

the night, while the Curé d'Ars was often dragged and thrown from his bed by Satan.

Diabolical obsession is the demonic attack on the mind of a person. Fr. Amorth notes this includes times "when one is assailed by obsessive, unconquerable thoughts that he absolutely cannot dismiss."[131] More frighteningly, these demonic attacks can also cause hallucinations. According to Fr. Amorth, "The objects of these hallucinations can be manifested as visions, as voices, or as rustlings; they can also appear as monstrous figures, horrifying animals, or devils."[132] Once again, this was something Padre Pio experienced when demons would try to attack the saint by mimicking his spiritual director's appearance and voice.

Diabolical infestation is a demonic attack focused on houses and objects in order to torment people. We saw a great example of infestation in the first half of the Wizard Clip case, when a family was tormented by flying objects, mysterious noises, and the destruction of their property. According to Fr. Amorth, "The most common reason exorcists are called to exorcise houses are the strange phenomena and noises heard in these places that cannot be humanly explained."[133]

Physical disturbances are immediate physical attacks on people by demonic entities. Unlike possession and vexation, there is no attack on the mind, and the demons do not control the body. These attacks can manifest as invisible entities striking a person or even as a sudden illness with no medical explanation. Again, as Fr. Amorth notes, Padre Pio also suffered such things, sometimes having his head punched and banged against the floor with no natural explanation. Fr. Amorth says that God may permit demons to bring

[131] Amorth, *The Devil Is Afraid of Me*, 113.

[132] Amorth, *An Exorcist Explains the Demonic*, 72.

[133] Ibid., 113.

about such physical evil "for [the] sanctification" of the people involved.[134]

Finally, *demonic dependence* is the willful surrender of someone to the will of the devil. Fr. Amorth notes that demonic dependency happens "when one voluntarily places himself, willingly and knowingly, and with total adhesion, to dependency on Satan and thus becomes a slave of Satan, solely to obtain some favors and human successes."[135] This is the classic Faustian bargain wherein someone sells his soul to gain fame, money, power, or some other markers of success.

Fr. Amorth learned from Fr. Amantini how to look out for these types of demonic attacks, and he continued to observe them in his many years as an exorcist. As you can see, Fr. Amorth didn't think anybody was immune from extraordinary demonic attacks, including saints. At the same time, Fr. Amorth continued to stress that people were at a far higher risk of temptation than any other kind of demonic attack.

If you are interested in either Fr. Amorth's life or the history of exorcisms, his books are worth a read, especially *Father Amorth: My Battle against Satan* and *The Devil Is Afraid of Me*. I also recommend the documentary *The Devil and Father Amorth*, which was directed by William Friedkin, the director of *The Exorcist*.

Fr. Amorth and his stories are part of an ongoing belief and tradition of spiritual warfare in the Catholic Church. Compared to the other topics we've covered, the late exorcist and his accounts are recent, but he still comes across like a priest from the distant past. I think the fact that he was so traditional and so recent, along with his humor and candor, is what makes his work captivating to

[134] Amorth, *Get Behind Me, Satan*, 21.
[135] Amorth, *The Devil Is Afraid of Me*, 114.

many people, even those who would normally not read about an exorcist. In the end, though, his most important message and legacy is his fearless attitude in the face of evil. Fr. Amorth always knew he was protected by God and His angels and saints, and he always felt reassured in the ultimate and definite victory of God over all the forces of evil.

St. Michael the Archangel

Chapter 4

Saints to Ward Off Evil

FR. GABRIELE AMORTH had a few favorite saints he turned to for protection and assistance in his work as an exorcist, including Mary, St. Gabriel, and Padre Pio. He also invoked St. Michael the Archangel and used a St. Benedict medal in his exorcisms, as most exorcists do. However, just about any saint can be a great patron for overcoming evil.

"As concerns the saints," Fr. Amorth said, "every exorcist invokes those to whom he is personally most devoted, or to whom the person he is assisting is most devoted."[136] If you are already devoted to a particular saint, you can always turn to him or her if you ever have to face something diabolical. In the traditions of the Catholic Church, though, there are certain saints people have long turned to for protection from evil spirits and other calamities.

St. Michael the Archangel, as we've seen, is a popular saint to call upon when we are faced with all kinds of dangers. He's a patron saint of military personnel, firefighters, and police officers, but he is also a protector of the Church and a powerful ally in facing evil. After all, St. Michael was the one who cast Lucifer from Heaven, so it is easy to see why the faithful regularly turn to him for overcoming danger, especially demonic danger.

[136] Amorth, *Get Behind Me, Satan*, 61.

St. Benedict of Nursia

Another popular yet possibly surprising saint whom people often invoke when facing evil is St. Benedict of Nursia. St. Benedict's most enduring legacy is his monastic rule and the establishment of the Benedictine order. St. Benedict is often thought of as the founder of Western Monasticism, and his monasteries became cultural treasure houses as the Roman Empire collapsed. But how did this peaceful monk and his medal come to be effective in keeping away evil? Even Fr. Amorth noted this oddness:

> St. Benedict was a monk, perhaps not even a priest, and for sure was not an exorcist. The reason for his identification as our patron lies in the fact that he was a great saint and demonstrated great vigor against the devil, given that he often drove him out, and his medal in particular has notable efficacy, as it contains many phrases against the Evil One.[137]

Most of what we know about St. Benedict comes from the *Dialogues* of Pope St. Gregory the Great. St. Benedict was born around 480 to a noble Roman family, and he was known for performing miracles from an early age. It was even said that the young Benedict could repair broken items simply by praying over them.

St. Benedict first went to Rome for his education but eventually moved to find a proper place for solitude and prayer. He lived as a hermit in Subiaco, where he would also establish a monastery, and he began to draw disciples to him. By the time St. Benedict died in 547, he had established several monasteries and had codified his rule of monastic life, which monks have continued to use up until today.

[137] Ibid.

The St. Benedict medal that many exorcists carry and use in their spiritual battles has prayers and symbols from the life of St. Benedict. It can be worn around the neck or incorporated into a crucifix, much like the crucifix used by Fr. Amorth in his work. This medal is thought to be a powerful weapon against demons because the saint's holiness and intercession torment the demons. The medal also includes many prayers of exorcism. One such powerful prayer is engraved around the rim on the back of the medal and is represented by the letters V R S N S M V – S M Q L I V B, which stands for this Latin prayer:

> Vade retro Satana!
> Nunquam suade mihi vana!
> Sunt mala quae libas.
> Ipse venena bibas!

This is translated:

> Begone, Satan,
> Do not suggest to me thy vanities!
> Evil are the things thou offerest,
> Drink thou thy own poison!

This prayer comes from the life of St. Benedict when the monks of Subiaco asked him to be their abbot. Some of the monks, who had been diabolically influenced, didn't like the idea of St. Benedict as their leader, and they tried to poison his bread and wine. The poisoned bread was carried off by a raven who saved the monk, and that is why St. Benedict is often depicted with a raven. Likewise, when St. Benedict blessed his wine, the chalice broke, and the saint knew he was about to be poisoned.

St. Joseph is another saint who is often called upon to keep away evil. In one of the prayers to St. Joseph, he is called "the terror of demons." This is best explained by author and priest Fr. Donald Calloway: "Saint Joseph's fatherhood has power. The devil hates that Jesus and Mary obeyed the loving directives of St. Joseph. Now, in Heaven, the intercessory power of St. Joseph poses a serious threat to the wiles of the devil and the devil knows it."[138] One saint who famously understood St. Joseph's intercessory power over evil was Bl. Bartolo Longo.

Bl. Bartolo Longo (1841–1926) came of age during the tumultuous nineteenth century in Italy. Italian nationalism and the dream of a united peninsula were growing, and by the time he entered university, Bl. Bartolo was among one of many men in Italy searching for truth. He was studying law at Naples when he attended his first séance, and he soon attended more séances and took a greater interest in the occult. But Bl. Bartolo was not satisfied with mediums, and he sought a way to contact spirits directly. To that end, he made the decision to consecrate himself to Satan in both will and spirit. The young man would soon suffer hallucinations, nightmares, and bouts of ill health.

[138] Fr. Donald H. Calloway, "St. Joseph: Terror of Demons," *Signs and Wonders*, April 24, 2020, https://sign.org/articles/st-joseph-terror-of-demons-187491.

Through the friendship and prayers of a professor and a Dominican priest, however, Bl. Bartolo reconciled with the Church and found peace. He formed a great love for the Holy Family, and he would eventually establish the Shrine of the Blessed Virgin of the Rosary of Pompei. Soon he would become known as the Apostle to the Rosary, and he encouraged praying the Rosary to anyone he met. He also prayed daily to St. Joseph, whose role as the Terror of Demons he especially emphasized, saying, "It is a great blessing for souls to be under the protection of the saint whose name makes demons tremble and flee."[139]

Of course, the Blessed Virgin Mary is also a powerful force against evil. Fr. Amorth loved Mary and often called upon her Immaculate Heart in his ministry. The exorcist notes, "Not by chance have painters and sculptors portrayed the Immaculate Conception as the crushing of the serpent's head, [an] image of the devil. How much more, then, is she a powerful intercessor."[140] Her prayers are crucial for anyone who has to face evil, and the image of her crushing the head of the Evil One is a powerful reminder of her strength.

In the end, we must remember that the saints are powerful spiritual friends who are constantly praying and interceding for us. Any saint can be a potent patron for protection from all kinds of dangers. The example of their holy lives and great deeds inspires us to live boldly and fearlessly in the face of both supernatural and everyday dangers. Through their intercessions, saints also provide the grace we need to withstand calamities, especially the weird ones we might encounter in life.

[139] Fr. Donald H. Calloway, *Consecration to St. Joseph* (Stockbridge, MA: Marian Press, 2019), 47.

[140] Amorth, *Get Behind Me, Satan*, 60.

Part 4

Unusual Miracles

"The most incredible thing about miracles is that they happen."

— G. K. Chesterton, *The Innocence of Father Brown*

HE GLOSSARY OF the *Catechism of the Catholic Church* defines miracles as "A sign or wonder, such as a healing or the control of nature, which can only be attributed to divine power."[141] Miracles are exceptions to the regular laws of nature, so by their definition, they are always strange and unusual, and in our post-Enlightenment era, we're likely to consider even the *possibility* of miracles to be strange.

We sometimes like to call any instance of good fortune miraculous, whether that's finding the best parking spot or getting approved for a new home. While these might be times when divine power does indeed intervene for us, they would not quite rank as miracles in the Catholic Church. That said, miracles don't have to be large displays of divine power, as we see in the miracles of Christ.

Christ did many great miracles throughout the Gospels, including raising the dead and healing people of various maladies. The Lord also performed smaller miracles, like turning water into wine and multiplying loaves and fishes to feed a multitude of people. As a modern reader, it's these smaller miracles that we might regard as *weird*. The comparison of the large and small miracles creates a sometimes humorous dichotomy, although each miracle is a wonder

[141] United States Conference of Catholic Bishops, *Catechism of the Catholic Church* (Baltimore: USCCB, 1999), 808.

in itself. Even as a devout Catholic, I would still use the word "weird" if I saw water turn into wine, as delighted as I would be.

We've already discussed some odd miracles from Catholic tradition, such as the monster fighters in the first section. Likewise, many Catholics would regard exorcism as a miraculous healing. We'll continue our exploration of unusual saints and miracles in this section of the book, although these miracles are only unusual in that they are unexpected, even by the standards of miracles. These miracles include stigmata, levitation, bilocation, and prophecy, the sort of things we don't often see, even in the Catholic Church's rich history of miracles. These phenomena especially stand out not only because they are rare, but also because they are dramatic examples of God's great power working through people.

We Still Believe in Miracles

The Catholic Church teaches that miracles are still possible and that they still occur in our day. These miracles are often associated with saints, and they are done not only for the sake of the people receiving them but also for those who witness or hear about them. According to Catholic teachings, miracles strengthen the faith of everyone by reinforcing divine power and revelation. The *Catechism* says,

> Thus the miracles of Christ and the saints, prophecies, the Church's growth and holiness, and her fruitfulness and stability "are the most certain signs of divine Revelation, adapted to the intelligence of all." (156)

Miracles are still important for Catholics and are a major part of our tradition. The lives of saints often include great miracles, and modern canonization still requires two verified miracles. You can find active

Catholic shrines that celebrate miracles all over the world. These shrines can be dedicated to big and small miracles and are a rich part of our Catholic heritage.

Not far from where I live, just outside of Golden, Colorado, is one such shrine that celebrates a miracle by the first United States citizen to be canonized a saint. St. Frances Xavier Cabrini, popularly known as Mother Cabrini, was an Italian saint who eventually immigrated to the United States as a missionary nun. She visited many

places in the Americas in pursuit of her mission, and one of those places she frequently visited was Colorado.

Mother Cabrini purchased land on Lookout Mountain in 1902 to serve as a farm and summer retreat for the orphans in her care. Just like now, the property was a beautiful retreat from the city with wonderful views of the Rocky Mountains. Unfortunately, it had no easy access to water, and the nuns had to bring water up from a nearby canyon. The sisters came to Mother Cabrini and told her about the water situation, and their dear superior told them not to worry. Mother Cabrini gave instructions, saying, "Lift that rock over there and start to dig. You will find water fresh enough to drink and clean enough to wash." The sisters obeyed their superior, and, to their surprise, they discovered a miraculous spring. That spring still flows today, and many pilgrims collect the water in hopes that it still can work miracles. It may seem like a small, inconsequential miracle, but it was not treated as anything but glorious by the nuns and other people devoted to Mother Cabrini.

Mother Cabrini brought about a few other small miracles in her lifetime, including finding another miraculous spring at a charity house she ran. Sometimes, the small miracle would involve finding money that seemed to materialize out of nowhere, which Mother Cabrini would use for her charitable work. Mother Cabrini's intercession also brought about grand miracles, but these little ones show how much she trusted God to do good things through her. The little miracles also present a truth held by many believers: nothing is too big or too small for God.

Mother Cabrini's Colorado miracle is worth discussing for two reasons. The first is because

I want to reflect on a small miracle before we move on to more tremendous miracles. While the saintly miracles we're about to discuss are larger and more dramatic than finding water on a mountain, we should always remember that all miracles are still glorious for the people receiving them and for those who witness the miraculous phenomena.

The second reason to discuss Mother Cabrini's Colorado miracle is because it's a good example of how we can find saintly miracles all around us. Colorado doesn't have the Catholic history of a place like Rome, where the Catholic Church has had thousands of years of stories about saints and their miracles. Still, you can find shrines dedicated to saintly miracles even in a place like Colorado, and I have a feeling there is a miraculous shrine near you. So while we're talking about tremendous and theatrical miracles, remember that there are many more small miracles in Catholic history, and a few might be close to you.

St. Francis of Assisi
receives the Stigmata.

Chapter 1

Stigmata: The Wounds of Christ

SIDE FROM THE Virgin Mary, St. Francis of Assisi might be the most recognizable and beloved saint in Catholic history. His statue is often found in gardens, where he is usually portrayed with a wolf at his side and birds listening to his sermons. His love of the sick, the suffering, and the destitute, along with his love of animals, makes St. Francis a popular patron saint, especially for eccentric writers who are trying to embrace the mysticism of their faith (like me).

St. Francis has been revered by people since his lifetime, so there are many stories and legends associated with the holy troubadour. Some of these legends are incorporated into his iconography, such as the tradition of the saint befriending the Wolf of Gubbio, which is a story that came out after he died. While the Wolf of Gubbio tale may be popular and shows the saint's love and control over wild beasts, the story that most often gets retold and depicted is how St. Francis received the wounds of Christ.

St. Francis often prayed and practiced penance in solitude, seeking to understand God in the quiet forests and caves that surrounded his Umbrian hometown. Yet as the saint aged and his health began to seriously affect him, pilgrims and curiosity seekers started to seek out St. Francis more, and he was often disturbed from his prayers. So in August of 1224, the saint set out to spend forty days in prayer and fasting to prepare for the Feast of St. Michael the Archangel.[142]

To make sure he had the necessary solitude, St. Francis made his way to the isolated mountain of La Verna with two of his companions. Although his companions would tend to his needs, St. Francis was able to have solitude for days on end. La Verna was given to St. Francis and his religious order by Count Orlando, who thought the secluded hermitage with a small chapel and monastic cells would be helpful for spiritual retreats. Due to his health, St. Francis and his companions had to go to La Verna by horse, something that was normally against the saint's dedication to poverty.

St. Francis was ever anxious about whether his actions were in accord with God's will, and so the saint asked God for a sign as he arrived to La Verna. The next day, as the saint exited his cell, he was greeted by the birds of La Verna who came up to him, one by one, to sing him a song of welcome. Still, the saint was anxious, and he told his companions that a demon was assaulting and tempting him each night.[143] And so St. Francis, full of inner turmoil, sought to pray and meditate on the Passion of Christ each day of his retreat. As his time on the mountain progressed, St. Francis identified more and more with the mysteries of Christ's Crucifixion and death.

One night, while in intense prayer and meditation, St. Francis had a vision that brought him both peace and discomfort. He saw a man with six angelic wings, whom he identified as a seraphim,

[142] Fr. Augustine Thompson, O.P., *Francis of Assisi: A New Biography* (Ithaca, NY: Cornell University Press, 2012), loc. 2400 of 6753, Kindle.

[143] Ibid., loc. 2407.

looking down at him with a consoling expression. Above the angel's fiery wings was a figure of the Crucifixion, with a man fastened to a cross. The look of the seraphim brought him peace and consolation in a way that even the birds could not. Meanwhile, the vision of the Cross terrified him. The saint wondered what this vision could mean, and he spoke about it with his companions the next day. St. Francis rarely shared his mystical visions, so this one must have affected him greatly.

After his vision of the angel, wounds began to appear on the body of St. Francis. He tried to conceal them from his companions, but they were hard to ignore, especially because they caused the saint great pain. On the palms of his hands and the tops of his feet were protruding bits of flesh that looked like nail heads. On the backs of his hands and the bottoms of his feet, on the other side of the wounds, were other wounds that looked like the points of nails. Another wound materialized on the side of St. Francis, which would bleed no matter how much it was treated. St. Francis of Assisi had received the holy stigmata.

The stigmata are the mystical appearance of Christ's Crucifixion wounds on someone's body. Although it is a physical manifestation, the source of the pains is a result of the inner life of the mystic who experiences them. In his biography on St. Francis, Fr. Augustine Thompson describes the stigmata as a mystical experience, saying, "These physical marks reproduced the very wounds of Christ, the same wounds on which Francis meditated daily. They were as painful physically as his inner trials were spiritually."[144]

St. Francis did not like to speak of his stigmata. The only time he mentioned them was in a letter of thanksgiving to God that he

[144] Ibid., loc. 2466.

St. Rita mystically receives a thorn wound from the crown of thorns.

penned close to the end of his life. That letter is one of many relics preserved in the saint's basilica in Assisi. Yet several of his followers and companions were aware of what had happened to the saint.

St. Francis is likely the first saint to have received the stigmata, but he was not the last. Another saint who experienced at least a partial stigmata was the fifteenth-century nun St. Rita of Cascia. St. Rita is a patron saint of impossible causes, and her life clearly demonstrated why she was assigned this patronage.

St. Rita was widowed, and she also lost her children. After these tragedies, she desired to become a nun, but she was turned away from the Augustinians in Cascia. So St. Rita sought her patron saints, Sts. Augustine, Nicholas of Tolentino, and John the Baptist, for help. Later that night, St. Rita had a vision of her three patrons. They assured her that she had a vocation, and they accompanied her to the Augustinian convent. There the patron saints unlocked the gates and doors, and St. Rita was found the next morning in the chapel. After the sisters heard how she got into the convent, they accepted her into their order.

St. Rita performed many miracles and had numerous visions throughout her vocation. Around the age of sixty, she heard a powerful sermon and asked God to help her join her sufferings to Christ. She had already suffered a lot in her life, but it seemed that God had one more cross for her to bear. She mystically received the crown of thorns from Christ's Crucifixion, which manifested on her in the form of a thorn wound on her forehead. The wound never healed; it continued until her death in 1457.

As if her mysticism in life weren't enough, St. Rita of Cascia was discovered to be one of the Incorruptibles when her tomb was opened in 1627.[145] Her partial stigmata was preserved along with

145 Cruz, *Incorruptibles*, 102.

the rest of her body. You can still view her saintly relics at her basilica in Cascia.

For both St. Francis of Assisi and St. Rita of Cascia, the stigmata were the fulfillment of their greatest desire, to be one with Christ. St. Francis often meditated on the Passion of Christ, reading and praying over the Gospels with great fervor, and the Passion was a major part of his sermons and writings. Likewise, St. Rita's experience of the stigmata was born from a moment of divine ecstasy. She had sought out union with Christ and wanted to share His experience. While the stigmata are physical manifestations of divine ecstasy, they are truly just a reflection of the deep, interior experience of divinity. Adam Blai, in his book *The Catholic Guide to Miracles*, echoes this point: "Stigmata are not the important thing but rather are indications that something more profound is already occurring."[146]

For modern readers, stigmata might be the most terrifying and unusual miracle. It might even feel debatable to call them a miracle. Most of us would not want to receive any new pains from God, as we probably have enough of our own, but some mystics sought union with Jesus so much that they wanted to experience all His pains so they could understand His peace and joy. And so from the perspective of a Catholic, the stigmata are indeed a miraculous occurrence, as they are a physical sign of interior union with Christ.

The stigmata also reflect one of the uncomfortable and hard teachings of the Catholic Church, the belief that suffering can be a way to make us holy. Suffering is unavoidable, but most of us either ignore it or dwell on it for too long. But the Catholic Church believes that suffering might just help us to become better people and can save our souls from sin. We need to be willing to bear our cross, just

[146] Blai, *Catholic Guide to Miracles*, 65.

as Christ did. There is also a sense of hope in this belief, because it helps us to find a way not to feel like helpless pawns. While suffering is as unfortunate as it is unavoidable, we have agency in how we react to suffering. Catholic Christians are called to identify our personal sufferings with the great suffering of Christ and to ask God for a way to still seek holiness through life's calamities. The Church promises that in uniting our sorrows with Christ's, we are rewarded with a mystical union with Christ, and we will therefore experience ecstasy beyond our comprehension.

Finally, while these stories are from centuries ago, stigmata are not just relics of the past. Some recent saints have also experienced the stigmata, such as Padre Pio (d. 1968) and St. Mary of Jesus Crucified, a Melkite Catholic saint and mystic who died in 1878. Even at this moment, it is possible that the Vatican is investigating a contemporary case of stigmata today.

While stigmata are among the most dramatic results of divine ecstasy, they are not the only physical phenomenon that comes from such union with Christ. Some saints have exuded mysterious lights or sweet smells with no known source. Others have experienced a supernatural power over their own human nature, such as the ability to consume nothing but the Eucharist for a long period of time. Divine ecstasy can also result in a miracle that might just be more amazing than stigmata: the miracle of levitation.

St. Joseph of Cupertino levitates during daily prayer.

Chapter 2

Levitation: When Saints Fly

VEN BEFORE HE began to float off the ground, St. Joseph of Cupertino just didn't fit in. He was born in 1603 in the Kingdom of Naples several months after his father died, and he was raised by a single mother who was often cruel to him. Due to his difficult childhood, young Joseph developed a violent temper. He also struggled in his studies, which gained him the scorn of his peers.

Despite his difficult childhood, or perhaps because of it, Joseph was a spiritual person who desired to become a priest. He had moments of divine ecstasy that often interrupted his work, and he was convinced that God was calling him to the Franciscans. When Joseph finished his studies, he applied to join the orders near him. The Franciscans rejected him due to his lack of education, so he sought out the Capuchins, who let him stay for a few months before ultimately rejecting him. His lack of education was an issue, but the friars also found him to be burdensome and unhelpful to the community, as his work kept getting interrupted by ecstasies that made him drop dishes or forget what he was doing.

Eventually, Joseph was able to find work with the Conventual Franciscans, also known as the Order of Friars Minor

Conventual, after he begged them to let him work in their stables. With the Conventual Franciscans, Joseph found work he could do well, and, through prayer and work, he managed to gain control over his wrathful temper as well as his clumsiness. The friars were impressed with his work and allowed him to formally join and study for the priesthood. He was ordained in 1628, and almost immediately afterward, his ecstasies began to manifest in levitations.

When he said Mass or prayed his daily prayers, St. Joseph of Cupertino would often float off the ground. Usually, he only floated a few inches or a foot above the ground. Still, this was a sight to behold, and people would come to see the floating friar pray. One witness was the Spanish ambassador who came to visit St. Joseph with his wife. At the sight of a statue of the Virgin Mary, St. Joseph floated about ten feet above the ambassador and a small crowd. After floating up, he flew to the statue and then to the door of the church. This was witnessed by several other people that day who later told consistent stories about the saint's levitation.[147]

Another notable witness to St. Joseph of Cupertino's levitations was none other than the pope. The friars and superiors of St. Joseph's order had an audience with Pope Urban VIII, who greeted the friars as they each came to pay him respect. At the time, it was customary for priests to kiss the foot of the pope. Yet after St. Joseph bent and kissed the pope's foot, he immediately levitated several feet into the air and only floated down when his superior ordered him to come down.[148] Many other

[147] Blai, *Catholic Guide to Miracles*, 111.
[148] Ibid., 112.

people also witnessed these levitations, as they had become a common occurrence.

Unfortunately, St. Joseph's spiritual ecstasies were causing problems for the friars. Curiosity seekers were becoming frequent, as many wanted to witness the levitations. Soon, St. Joseph also attracted the attention of the Inquisition, who worried that he was using witchcraft or some other form of sorcery. The Inquisition placed St. Joseph in seclusion at a remote monastery with his own private cell and chapel, and he was forbidden even to eat with the other friars. St. Joseph lived in this seclusion for several years until the Inquisition was satisfied that he was not engaged in any form of devilry. After his forceful seclusion was ended, St. Joseph continued to pray and work, and he had moments of divine ecstasy until he died on September 18, 1663.

As we found with the stigmata, levitation was the product of St. Joseph's interior life. He was not what most people think of when they think of a saint, but he still desired union with Christ and prayed for that closeness daily. Despite his difficulties, nothing could stop St. Joseph from seeking out a deeper relationship with Christ, and few things could halt the incredible joy he felt in these moments. For St. Joseph of Cupertino, levitation was the physical manifestation of his interior movement toward Jesus.

Other saints and mystics have also been known to levitate during moments of divine ecstasy. St. Teresa of Ávila, one of the most influential mystics in history, was known to levitate during her prayers and meditations, and she even wrote about this experience in her spiritual autobiography.[149] St. Philip Neri — sometimes called the "Socrates of Rome" for his habit of walking and engaging people in conversation — was also

[149] Ibid., 109.

witnessed levitating a few inches off the ground when he was ecstatic. Another saint known to levitate was St. Mary of Jesus Crucified, who also experienced many other types of mystical phenomena in her lifetime.

The saints of Catholic history who experienced levitation often also had other mystical experiences when they were in divine ecstasy. While all of these miraculous experiences are noteworthy, levitation still stands out, especially because it feels so theatrical. Everyone has a dream in which they can fly, but some saints actually get to experience it. Levitation simply defies the law of gravity. It is a sign of God's power over nature, and the people who witness it are often struck in disbelief.

The other reason why levitation stands out among so many mystical miracles is because it is fairly difficult to fake. There have always been charlatans and tricksters who prey on religious believers, and many of them are not above faking a miracle. As such, there is always a level of skepticism required when reading about miracles, even from an orthodox Catholic perspective. However, of all the miracles out there, levitation is one of the most difficult to fake and easiest to disprove. If St. Joseph of Cupertino had just been using clever rigs and fishing lines, then he would not have been able to perform such a miracle in different places and in front of so many various people.

Again, we must emphasize that while miracles like levitation provide for dramatic accounts and incredible stories, they are always secondary to what is truly going on within the saint. St. Joseph of Cupertino and St. Teresa of Ávila were not declared saints because they could fly. They were declared saints because of their great holiness, especially in the face of difficult circumstances, and because of their pious works. Miracles like levitation simply serve as confirmation of the saint's holiness and union with Christ.

So while a miracle like levitation may draw our imaginations, it's best to remember that miracles always result from God working through His saints.

St. Padre Pio, who performed
the miracle of bilocation

Chapter 3

St. Padre Pio: A Saint in Two Places at Once

IF WE USE the definition of *weird* that I've been using throughout this book, that is, something strange or unusual, I don't think anyone is a better example of a weird Catholic figure than St. Pio of Pietrelcina, also known as Padre Pio. As I've consistently done in this book, I call him weird in the most affectionate way I can. Padre Pio was weird because he was like a medieval mystic who was taken from his own time and moved into the middle of the twentieth century. Sometimes, when I'm reading about him, I imagine him more like a man living in the age of St. Francis of Assisi than in a time of cars and televisions. However, he is a real saint, and he is beloved by millions of people in and out of the Catholic Church.

I've discussed Padre Pio a few times in this book because the Italian saint experienced so many of the phenomena we've discussed. Padre Pio was the longtime spiritual director of the exorcist Fr. Gabriele Amorth, and the saint often experienced his own spiritual battles. Padre Pio was attacked by demons in several ways, and he assisted in delivering people from demonic torment by sending those needing help to the sanctuary on Monte Gargano, the site of a St. Michael apparition we discussed at the beginning of this book.[150]

[150] Ibid., 59.

The mystic and saint also received the stigmata, and he performed many other miracles in his life and after his death. And so, in so many ways, Padre Pio fits nicely into our little collection of weird stories from Catholic history.

St. Pio was born Francesco Forgione on May 25, 1887, in Campania to two devout parents. By the age of five, the young Francesco knew he wanted to dedicate his life to Christ. Although it required some sacrifices from his parents, he studied hard during his youth, despite some health problems that would affect him throughout his life. At the age of fifteen, Francesco joined the Capuchin novitiate in 1903. Later that same year, he took vows and the Capuchin habit and assumed the religious name Pio. He was ordained in 1910.

Padre Pio had moments of divine ecstasy throughout his life, and people witnessed many miracles when he went into these ecstasies. He also struggled with various health ailments, some severe, during his life. Many great books about Padre Pio can go more in-depth on his incredible life and miracles than I can, but there are a few miracles that are worth discussing. His most inspiring miracles are certainly the ones in which his intercession brought healing to the sick, but we'll discuss some of his most unusual miracles here.

One of the miracles Padre Pio performed was bilocation. As the name implies, bilocation occurs when a person is able to be in two places at once. Several saints, going back to the Virgin Mary, have manifested the miracle of bilocation, but Padre Pio might be the most famous of saints who is associated with this miracle. Fr. Carmelo Durante, his religious superior, testified that Padre Pio met with him while the friar was also meeting with others at the same time, sometimes even visiting a spiritual child of his in America.[151]

[151] "Padre Pio's Bilocation and the Odor of Sanctity," *EWTN Religious Library*, accessed June 30, 2024, https://www.ewtn.com/catholicism/library/padre-pios-bilocation-and-the-odor-of-sanctity-13853.

Padre Pio's most dramatic appearance happened in the air over his town during World War II. At the time, southern Italy was occupied by the Nazis, and the Allies were bombing military targets. Padre Pio promised the people of his town, San Giovanni Rotondo, that the town would be spared. One day, some American planes were set to bomb San Giovanni Rotondo, but they failed to release their munitions. Some of the pilots reported seeing a brown-robed friar in the air. After the war, one of the pilots visited Padre Pio to see the man who appeared midair on that fateful day.[152]

Another miraculous ability possessed by Padre Pio was his gift of being able to communicate with angels, including not only his own guardian angel but also other people's guardian angels. Padre Pio often told people to rely on their guardian angels, since our guardian angel is always praying for us. As he said in one letter:

> This heavenly spirit guides and protects us like a friend, a brother. But it is very consoling to know that this angel prays unceasingly for us, and offers God all of our good actions, our thoughts, and our desires, if they are pure.[153]

The mystic would also tell people who lived far from him to send him their guardian angels, saying, "Do not move if you have something to tell me, but send me your angel! He does not pay for any train tickets."[154]

Once, a busload of pilgrims was making their way to San Giovanni Rotondo at night when a massive storm hit. Some of the pilgrims remembered that Padre Pio often said to send their angels,

[152] Ibid.

[153] Odile Haumonté, *Encounters with Angels*, trans. James Henri McMurtrie (Manchester, NH: Sophia Institute Press, 2021), 110.

[154] Ibid., 27.

and they did just that, asking their guardian angels for prayer and to carry an urgent message to the friar. The pilgrims made it safely to their destination, and when they got off the bus, they found Padre Pio waiting to meet them. The holy priest exclaimed, "My children, you woke me up last night. I had to pray for you."[155] This ability to talk with angels often meant the saint knew things about people that they thought were hidden, which was a surprise to many of his spiritual children.

When he celebrated Mass, Padre Pio would often become contemplative and even experience divine ecstasy at the words of consecration for the Eucharist. In these moments, some perceived him to be levitating just a few inches off the ground. He also would see angels gathering around the altar during Mass while in these ecstasies. When someone asked who he saw at the altar, he simply said, "The whole celestial court."[156]

The mystical friar tried to bear his own personal sufferings and health complications with grace, and he offered his sufferings for the salvation of others. At one point he began feeling the pains of the wounds of Christ, but at first they left no marks on his body. Then, in 1918, he had a vision of a seraph angel who left marks of the wounds of Christ on his hands, feet, and side.[157] Padre Pio would live with his stigmata for fifty years.

Padre Pio died on September 23, 1968, at the age of eighty-one. He was considered a saint by many people in his lifetime, and the cause for his canonization was opened soon after his death. He was beatified in 1992 and canonized in 2002 by Pope St. John Paul II. He is still beloved by millions throughout the

155 Ibid., 28.
156 Ibid., 104.
157 Ibid., 237.

world, and he's the namesake of several ministries, shrines, and parishes on multiple continents.

As with other miracles we've discussed, the miracles that surrounded Padre Pio were the result of his interior desire for union with Christ. He frequently spent time in prayer and meditation and experienced several moments of divine ecstasy. While many spoke of his miracles, more people spoke of his kindness and spiritual wisdom. The miracles were always only a reflection of his spiritual state, as he had a heart for charity and saw to the needs of those who suffered physical and spiritual ailments. As I said earlier, St. Pio of Pietrelcina feels to me like a medieval mystic plopped into our time, and I have a feeling that people will be telling the story of Padre Pio for generations to come, just like the legends and tales of the medieval mystics.

The Miraculous Staircase built by St. Joseph
Loretto Chapel, Santa Fe, New Mexico

Chapter 4

St. Joseph's Miraculous Staircase

E'VE DISCUSSED SOME fantastic and dramatic miracles, but as I've said before, miracles don't have to be over the top to still be wondrous and incredible. As we end our journey in this book, let us take a look at one small but amazing miracle that may be a little closer to home.

Santa Fe, New Mexico, has a long history of Catholicism compared to other U.S. cities. It is home to one of the oldest Catholic churches in the nation, the San Miguel Mission, as well as many other historic parishes and buildings. One of these treasured buildings is the Loretto Chapel, a beautiful, neo-Gothic church that was built in 1878 by the Loretto Sisters for their new school and for their community's daily religious services.

The story goes that the chapel was nearing completion and was just about perfect except for one thing: there was no easy access to the choir loft. In traditional Gothic architecture, there would be ladders to reach the loft, but this wouldn't work for the nuns. Unfortunately, most carpenters said they couldn't build a staircase without considerable expense and space. Not sure what to do, the sisters and students prayed a novena to the patron saint of carpenters, St. Joseph, the husband of Mary and the earthly father of Jesus.

St. Joseph's novena has been a powerful tool for many Catholics throughout history. It is prayed every morning for nine days, often during difficult situations like unemployment or poor health, or, in the case of the Sisters of Loretto, when there seems to be an impossible difficulty. St. Joseph's intercession is powerful, so many people undertake his novena to find comfort and help in hard times.

On the final day of the novena, a man with a donkey and some tools came to the Loretto Chapel to offer his services. When the sisters told him of their ordeal, he promised that he could build a suitable staircase for them. The stranger got to work and built a beautiful helix-shaped spiral staircase. Remarkably, the spiral staircase didn't have a center pole for support and was self-supporting. It is a remarkable work of carpentry and is still a beautiful feature of the chapel.

The stranger departed before the nuns could pay or thank him, and so they asked other carpenters who he might be, but nobody had a clue who he was. They even took an ad out in the local newspaper to try to find the carpenter, but to no avail. The Sisters of Loretto never found the kind stranger and soon concluded that it was St. Joseph himself who came to answer the prayer by building a masterpiece of carpentry with his own hands.

The Sisters of Loretto eventually left their chapel and closed down their school, and the Loretto Chapel is now a private museum and wedding venue. Carpenters and architects have studied the miraculous staircase, and pilgrims still come to see it. Although this story is more akin to folklore than a Church-approved miracle, it still inspires wonder and awe.

While a saint building a staircase is not as exciting of a miracle compared to levitation, bilocation, or stigmata, the Sisters of Loretto were still thankful to have received it. The sisters had a practical need that they couldn't meet, and St. Joseph seemed to hear their prayers and solve their problem with a practical miracle. And the idea of a saint stepping down from Heaven to do some miraculous carpentry is still a wondrous and astounding thing to consider.

Many people still believe that St. Joseph built this spiral staircase, but, of course, it's understandable to feel skepticism when hearing this story. Even people who love St. Joseph and believe in his intercession would likely want more definitive proof of divine intervention before declaring this a miracle, and that is a good thing. As we saw with the Incorruptibles and other miracles, the Catholic Church researches and explores all possible explanations before declaring anything a miracle. Perhaps this event was all coincidence, and maybe the sisters' prayers were answered by a charitable local who happened to be a master carpenter. It's a possibility we can't fully rule out. Still, there are also other factors that believers point to when they declare this staircase miraculous. One of the things that believers will point to is the incredible craftsmanship and the exotic wood used in constructing the staircase. The wood seemed to be imported and not from a local lumber yard, which just adds to the mysterious nature of the staircase.

However, the main point of this story for us and for the sisters is that their prayers were answered. Whether it was St. Joseph who built the staircase or not, the sisters prayed a novena, and they had a new staircase thanks to the intercession of St. Joseph. Given all that we've explored, it's not that strange to imagine a saint making an appearance to those who needed him, but regardless of who actually built the staircase, the story encourages a deep prayer life and devotion to the saints.

St. Joseph is a popular saint, and his novena is said to be a powerful prayer. I also have a devotion to St. Joseph and have prayed the novena several times, and I find it a beautiful and peaceful prayer, especially when I'm in a bind. So as you can imagine, I want this story to be true, even as I have a few questions about it. It's inspiring and hopeful, and I'm glad it is still being shared.

Catholic beliefs about saints and their ability to intercede for us are at the heart of this story about the miraculous staircase of St. Joseph. In the Catholic Church, the saints are called upon for great and little miracles every day. The miracles that God brings about through His saints include levitation and the power to bring monsters to heel or to cast out demons, but they may also include a saintly carpenter answering your humble and prayerful request. These and other weird events in the history of the Church inspire us to have faith, no matter what monsters and evils we face. The miraculous stories that Catholics tell, from mysterious stairs in New Mexico to the Resurrection of the Dead, express a supernatural hope that we can endure through any challenge. As Catholics, we believe that even death itself will be defeated, and so a miraculous staircase can seem odd or insignificant. However, all these weird tales from Catholic history show the fundamental beliefs Catholics have held about God's place in our life and our death. All these tales speak to a larger story, the story of God's work throughout human history to bring us into a better world than the one we currently occupy. Seeing this story play out in monstrous legends, ghostly folklore, old crypts, and unusual miracles is one of the delights of learning about the history of our faith.

Part 5

A Weird Catholic Pilgrimage

E'VE EXPLORED SOME incredible stories from Catholic history as well as some strange and unusual places of pilgrimage. Of course, there are many more places to explore and saintly stories to tell. We could even dive deeper into the stories and people we've discussed in this short book. If you've made it this far, however, I hope you are ready to go on your own weird Catholic pilgrimage.

There is a good chance that you already have a list of pilgrimage destinations in mind, and I hope you're able to take at least one such pilgrimage in your lifetime. However, many of the places we've discussed in this book are not too far from traditional pilgrimage sites. With just a little planning, you can visit St. Peter's Basilica in Rome or the Infant of Prague and also take a pilgrimage to some odd or overlooked places of Catholic history.

To help you find a weird Catholic pilgrimage of your own, I have put together some places you can add to your next journey. Many of these spots were discussed in this book, which will make visiting them all the more endearing for you as seeing them will give you more experience and insight into the themes we've explored. However, there are also sites on this list that I didn't include in this book but certainly could have. I have had the pleasure of seeing a few of these places in person, but I still have not visited the majority of those listed below. Where I can, however, I will give my observations as somebody who has seen these weird and wonderful sites.

A list of weird, overlooked, and strange places of pilgrimage would be hard to complete, and, as such, this list is incomplete. I do not doubt that there are places I have missed despite my desire to find overlooked sacred spaces. There is a strong chance that you have a forgotten shrine or pilgrimage site in mind that you could add to this list. If you do, I pray that it becomes a place that touches more hearts for generations to come. A pilgrimage is never walked alone, and it is a joy to share these strange sacred places with others.

Throughout this book, I've encouraged you to think of overlooked Catholic sites near you. I myself have been surprised at what I can find here in Colorado. As Catholics, it's so easy to think that Church history ends at the Italian border, but it's so much more than that. The events of the Catholic past unfolded around us too, and they will continue to do so. We participate in Catholic history just as our spiritual ancestors did. If you can find a forgotten or unusual shrine, church, or saint near you, make a plan to see it and read up on its history. It might surprise you how often the histories of your locality and your faith coincide with one another.

This list is a good starting point for creating a weird Catholic pilgrimage. You'll also learn more about the saints and places we've mentioned in this book by visiting them and similar sites. Wherever you decide to start, you have many patron saints who can look over your future journey.

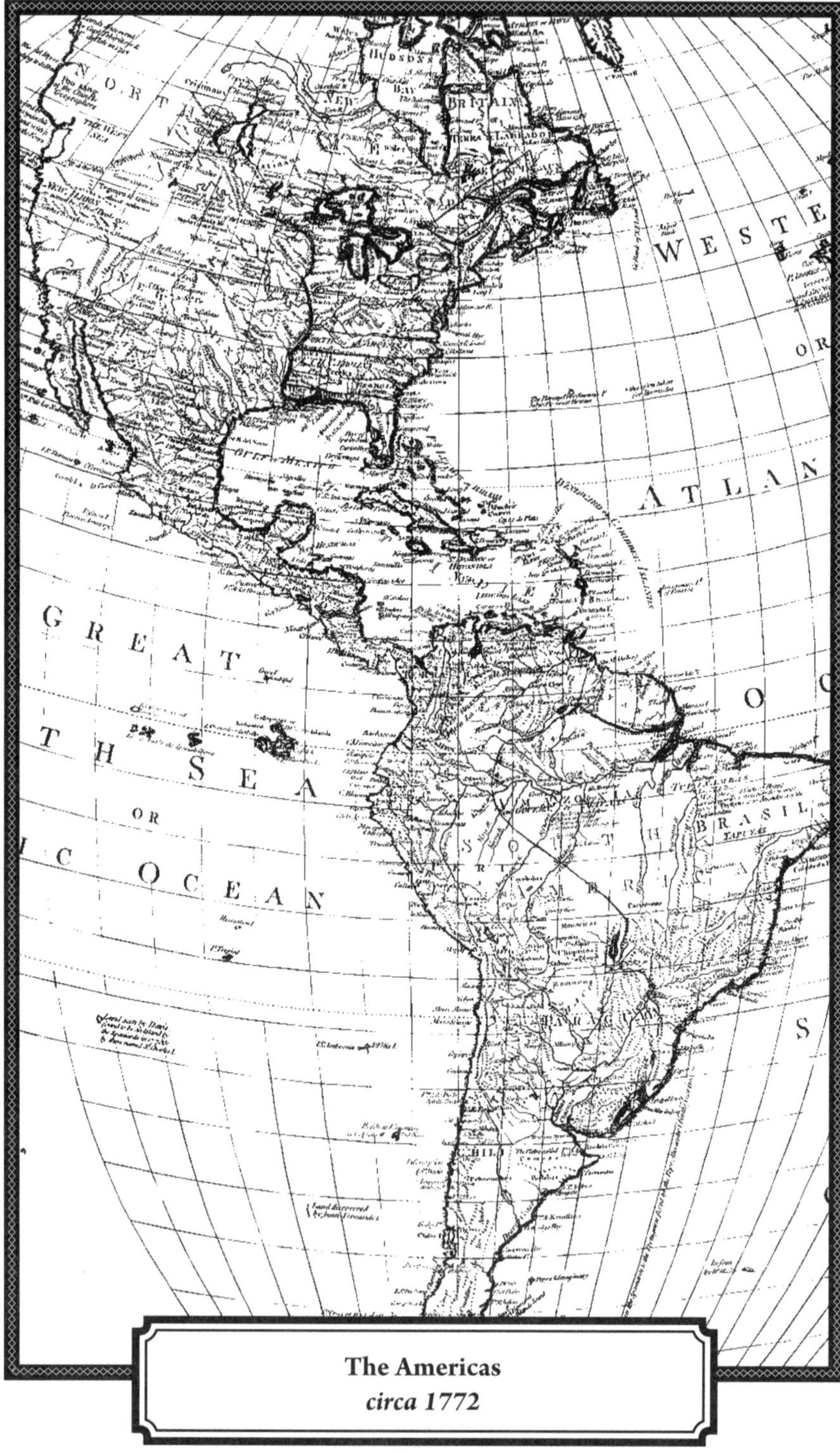

The Americas
circa 1772

The Americas

1. **Santuario Nacional de San Miguel Arcángel**
   No. 58 San Miguel del Milagro, 90720 Natívitas, Tlaxcala, Mexico
   The church celebrates a 1631 apparition of St. Michael the Archangel during an outbreak of disease.

2. **Basilica and Convent of Santo Domingo**
   Jirón Camaná 170, Jirón Conde de Superunda 262, Lima, Peru
   https://conventosantodomingo.pe/
   St. Rose of Lima, a mystic and Incorruptible, is buried in this basilica, along with St. Martin de Porres. A little more of a traditional pilgrimage site, but I thought it fit here still.

3. **Basilica and Convent of San Francisco**
   Plaza San Francisco, Lima, Peru
   https://museocatacumbas.com/
   Beneath the old Franciscan monastery are the catacombs of Lima, which is home to what may be the only ossuary in the Western Hemisphere.

4. **Benedictines of Mary Queen of Apostles, Abbey of Our Lady of Ephesus**
   8005 NW 316th Street, Gower, Missouri
   https://benedictinesofmary.org/
   The Benedictine sisters record and sing beautiful music, and the abbey is the burial place of their founder, Sr. Wilhelmina Lancaster, who may be the first Incorruptible from the United States and the first African American Incorruptible.

5. **Old St. Ferdinand Shrine**
   1 Rue St. Francois Street, Florissant, Missouri
   https://www.oldstferdinandshrine.org/
   An early nineteenth-century missionary church and shrine that now operates as a museum and event venue. They host religious pilgrims, as they have a relic of St. Valentine, and the grounds are associated with St. Rose Philippine Duchesne.

6. **The Loretto Chapel**
   207 Old Santa Fe Trail, Santa Fe, New Mexico
   https://www.lorettochapel.com/
   A neo-Gothic chapel with a beautiful spiral staircase that is said to have been built by St. Joseph. It's a private museum and wedding chapel, so check the website for opening hours.

7. **Basilica of St. Michael the Archangel**
   321 St. Mary Street, Loretto, Pennsylvania
   https://www.basilicasm-loretto.org/
   A beautiful basilica that was founded by Servant of God Demetrius Augustine Gallitzin, a missionary priest who is buried in the basilica's cemetery. Fr. Gallitzin is a major figure in early U.S. Catholic history, and he witnessed the Wizard Clip haunting.

8. **Saint Anthony Chapel**
   1704 Harpster Street, Pittsburgh, Pennsylvania
   https://pghshrines.org/about-st-anthony-chapel
   The largest collection of relics you can find outside the Vatican. Usually open in the afternoons, but check their website for updated hours.

9. **Priest Field Pastoral Center**
   4030 Middleway Pike, Kearneysville, West Virginia
   https://priestfield.org/
   A Catholic retreat center on land that was donated by Adam Livingston after priests helped deliver his family from the Wizard Clip haunting. The nearby town of Middleway has markers on other sites associated with the haunting.

10. **The Mother Cabrini Shrine**
    20189 Cabrini Blvd, Golden, Colorado
    https://mothercabrinishrine.org/
    The Mother Cabrini Shrine is built on land that was originally a summer camp and farm for St. Frances Xavier Cabrini's orphanage. It sits on the side of Lookout Mountain, just outside of Denver, and features a miraculous spring associated with Mother Cabrini. The water from that miraculous spring is collected by pilgrims for holy water or directly consumed.

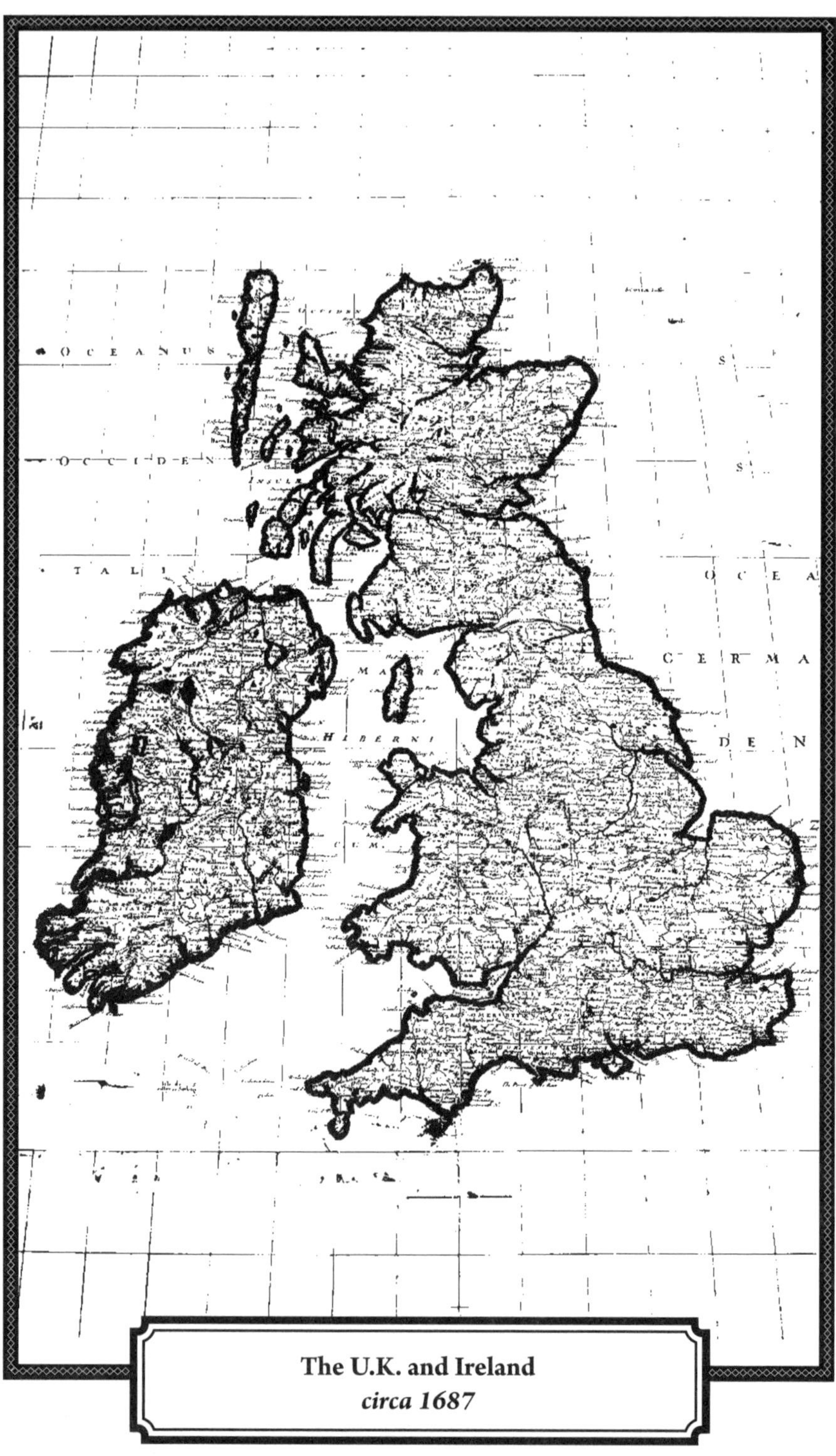

The U.K. and Ireland
circa 1687

The United Kingdom and Ireland

1. **St. Leonard's Church**
   3 Oak Walk, Hythe CT21 5DN, United Kingdom
   https://www.slhk.org/theossuary.htm
   A small ossuary lies beneath this medieval church. It tends to only be open in the summers, so do some research before heading out.

2. **Dragon Hill, Uffington**
   Faringdon SN7 7QH, United Kingdom
   Near the prehistoric Uffington White Horse, it is said that grass will not grow on this hill after St. George killed a dragon on top of it.

3. **Lough Derg and St. Patrick's Purgatory**
   County Donegal, Ireland
   https://www.loughderg.org/
   St. Patrick came to this lake and slew the ancient serpent that lived in it. It is on one of the islands in an ancient pilgrimage site that was also the entrance to St. Patrick's Purgatory.

4. **Croagh Patrick**
   County Mayo, Ireland
   A mountain where St. Patrick confronted old and dark spirits before he was able to overcome them with his sacred bell. On the last Sunday in July, Reek Sunday, pilgrims climb the mountain, some walking up to twenty-one miles with no shoes.

5. **St. Michan's Church**
   Church St, Arran Quay, Dublin 7, D07 F3P6, Ireland
   http://www.cathedralgroupdublin.ie/
   An old church whose crypt is home to accidentally mummified bodies. Famous visitors are said to include Bram Stoker. Hours are a little weird, so check before making a trip.

6. **Whitefriar Street Church**
   56 Aungier St, Dublin 2, D02 YF57, Ireland
   https://whitefriarstreetchurch.com/
   A beautiful Carmelite church in the center of Dublin. It famously has a relic of St. Valentine, and couples often go there to pray when discerning marriage.

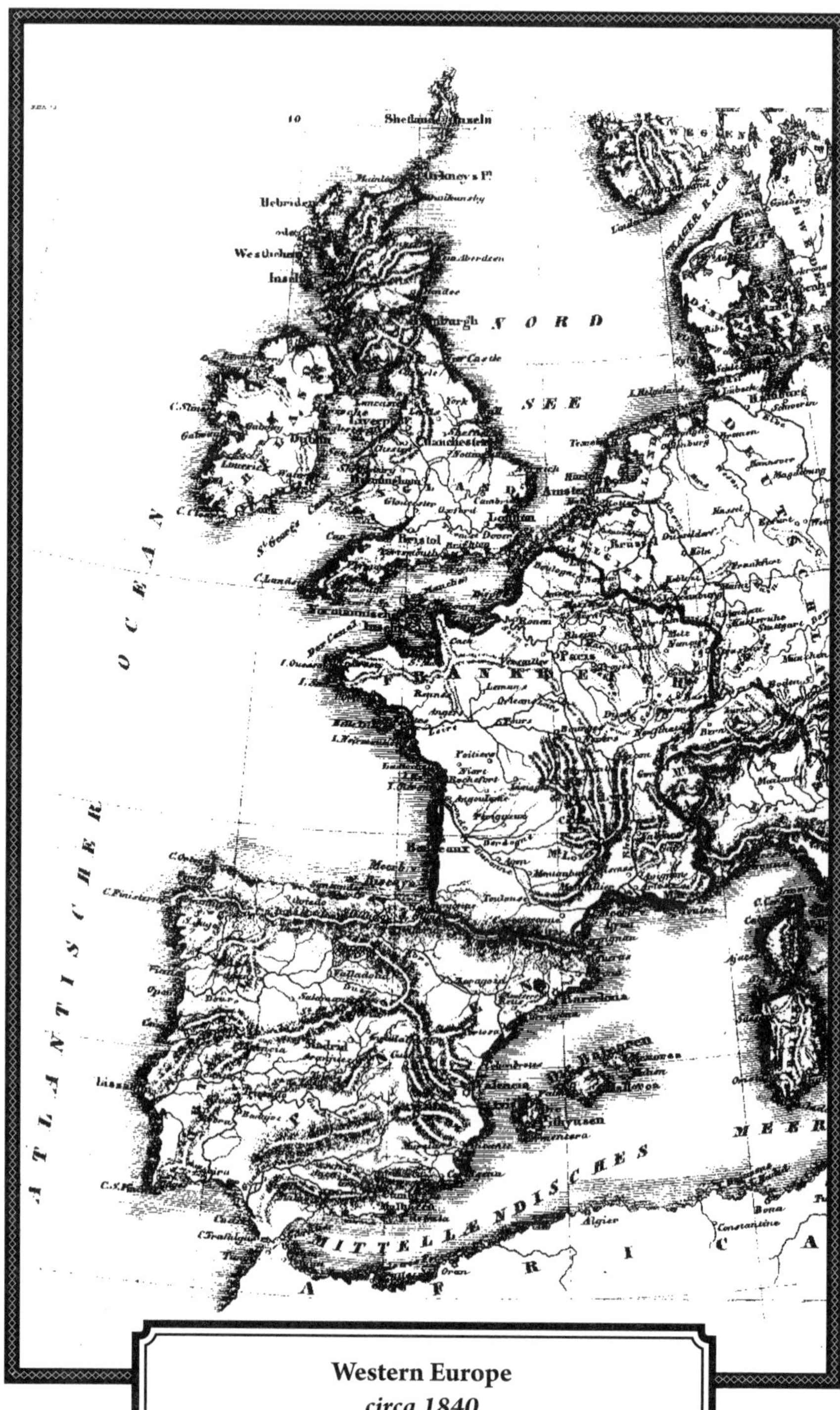

Western Europe
circa 1840

Western Europe

1. **Aitre Saint-Maclou**
   186 Rue Martainville, 76000 Rouen, France
   https://www.aitresaintmaclou.fr/en/
   The site of an ancient ossuary is now a museum and event space. Worth stopping by to see some incredible danse macabre *imagery.*

2. **Notre-Dame de l'Assomption de Rouen**
   Place de la Cathédrale, 76000 Rouen, France
   https://www.cathedrale-rouen.net/
   A beautiful cathedral that is featured in a couple of Monet paintings. Look out for a statue of St. Romanus of Rouen, a saint and dragonslayer.

3. **St. Joseph des Carmes**
   70 Rue de Vaugirard, 75006 Paris, France
   https://www.sjdc.fr/
   The church crypt displays the bones of martyrs who died during the French Revolution.

4. **Capela dos Ossos**
   Praça 1º de Maio 4, 7000-650 Évora, Portugal
   https://igrejadesaofrancisco.pt/
   Beneath the monastery of São Francisco is an ossuary decorated with thousands of bones.

5. **Capela dos Ossos de Faro**
   Largo do Carmo 21, 8000-148 Faro, Portugal
   A small ossuary made from the bones of Carmelite monks.

Central Europe
circa 1981

Central Europe

1. **Hallstatt Charnel House**
   Friedhof 164, 4830 Hallstatt, Austria
   A charnel house near the St. Michael chapel displays hundreds of bones and painted skulls.

2. **Melk Abbey**
   Abt-Berthold-Dietmayr-Straße 1, 3390 Melk, Austria
   https://www.stiftmelk.at/en/
   Melk Abbey is a triumph of baroque art and architecture and is worth a visit in itself. While in the abbey church, look out for St. Friedrich, a richly decorated catacomb saint. You can get to Melk Abbey from Vienna by boat, bus, or even a bicycle if you're feeling more adventurous.

3. **Kaisergruft (The Imperial Crypt)**
   Tegetthoffstraße 2, 1010 Vienna, Austria
   https://www.kapuzinergruft.com/
   The Capuchin Crypt is the traditional burial place of the Habsburg emperors, princesses, and other royals. The history is fascinating, and there is some incredible funerary work depicting memento mori.

4. **Brno Ossuary**
   Jakubské náměstí, 658 78 Brno-střed, Czechia
   https://podzemibrno.cz/en/
   An incredible ossuary beneath the Church of St. James that was only recently rediscovered. Some of the bones show signs of plague and also the earliest bullet wounds.

5. **Capuchin Crypt of Brno**
   Kapucínské náměstí 303/5, 602 00 Brno, Czechia
   https://hrobka.kapucini.cz/
   The crypt beneath the Holy Cross Church naturally mummified the friars and benefactors buried there. The crypt is a true spiritual experience and one of the most incredible opportunities for meditating on memento mori.

6. **Sedlec Ossuary**
   Zámecká, 284 03 Kutná Hora 3, Czechia
   https://www.sedlec.info/
   Arguably the most famous ossuary in the world. It's an easy trip from Prague, but I recommend coming early to avoid the busloads of tourists that come in the afternoon. Also, the town of Kutna Hora has incredible churches that are worth seeing after your trip to the ossuary. Both the nearby abbey church and St. Barbara's Cathedral are treasures of Czech art and architecture.

7. **Basilica of St. Ursula**
   Ursulapl. 24, 50668 Köln, Germany
   https://www.katholisch-in-koeln.de/
   Cologne has several beautiful churches, including St. Ursula's Basilica. Inside this basilica is the Golden Chamber, which preserves and displays the bones of thousands of martyrs.

8. **Roggenburg Abbey**
   Klosterstraße 5, 89297 Roggenburg, Germany
   https://www.kloster-roggenburg.de/
   A stunning baroque abbey in Bavaria with several catacomb saints. The catacomb saints are kept hidden except on the Feast of the Assumption (August 15), when they are decorated and taken on procession.

9. **Kaplica Czaszek (Skull Chapel)**
Stanisława Moniuszki 8a, 57–350 Kudowa-Zdrój, Poland
https://www.czermna.pl/
A centuries-old ossuary beneath St. Bartholomew's Church.

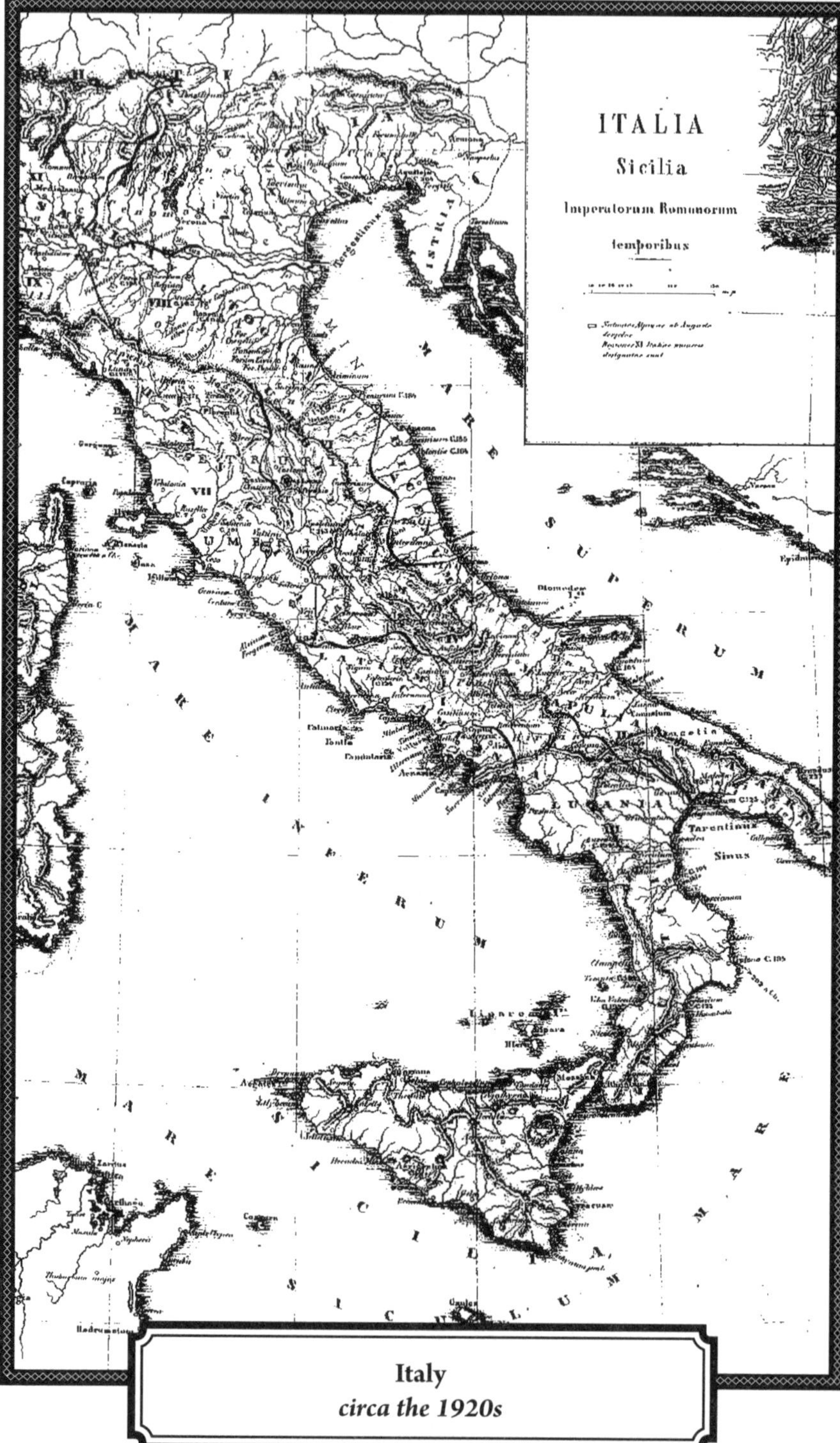

Italy
circa the 1920s

Italy

1. **San Filippo Neri**
   Via Vittorio Emanuele II, 10023 Chieri, Torino, Italy
   St. John Bosco attended the adjoining seminary where he experienced a visit from his departed friend, Luigi Comollo. Luigi is buried inside the church, where there is also a memorial to him and St. John Bosco.

2. **San Bernardino alle Ossa**
   Piazza Santo Stefano, 20122 Milano, Italy
   https://www.sanbernardinoalleossa.it/
   The small ossuary inside San Bernardino is also decorated with stunning frescoes. Unlike the other ossuaries on this list, you might actually have it to yourself. It is a great place to pray and meditate. Check the hours before visiting, and drop a donation for the upkeep before entering.

3. **Santuario di San Michele Arcangelo**
   Via Reale Basilica, 127, 71037 Monte Sant'Angelo FG, Italy
   https://www.santuariosanmichele.it/
   The sanctuary on Monte Gargano celebrates an apparition of St. Michael the Archangel. The site is also associated with the ministry of exorcism, with Padre Pio sending people here who needed spiritual assistance.

4. **Basilica di Santa Cecilia in Trastevere**
   Piazza di Santa Cecilia, 22, 00153 Roma, Italy
   http://www.benedettinesantacecilia.it/
   One of Rome's great churches is dedicated to St. Cecilia, an early Christian martyr and the most famous Incorruptible saint. Her incorruptible body was reproduced in a statue by Maderno, which is at the altar.

5. **Museo delle Anime del Purgatorio**
   Lungotevere Prati, 12, 00193 Roma, Italy
   Inside the church of Chiesa di Sacro Cuore di Gesù in Prati is a small collection called the Museum of the Souls in Purgatory. This includes things like books and banknotes that have hand and finger marks burnt into them by purgatorial souls who visited the living. Like many churches in Rome, it is usually closed in the afternoon, so look up the hours before visiting.

6. **Santa Maria della Concezione dei Cappuccini**
   Via Vittorio Veneto, 27, 00187 Roma, Italy
   https://museoecriptacappuccini.it/
   The Capuchin Crypt of Rome hosts an old and famous ossuary that inspired other ossuaries on this list. It has been visited by Mark Twain, Nathaniel Hawthorne, the Marquis de Sade, and many other well-known writers. An attached museum also tells the story of the Capuchin order in Rome. Because the ossuary is so popular, I strongly suggest coming here on a weekday morning so you can have some time to truly stop and wonder at the elaborate decorations of bones.

7. **Santa Maria dell'Orazione e Morte**
   Via Giulia, 262, 00186 Roma, Italy
   A church in Rome that took on the responsibility of burying abandoned bodies in Rome. It is decorated with skulls and other motifs of memento mori. *There is also a small ossuary.*

List of Illustrations

Christian Werewolves pg. 32: Indian asian old man having knee pain (1865930266), image derived from Image bug/shutterstock.com; Full moon and cloud (2262735803), image derived from Dancake/ shutterstock.com; Black Wolf (2207608799), image derived from evanesa/shutterstock.com; Charles Bianchini, a Franciscan Monk; costume design for Jeanne d'Arc by the Paris Opera Company, 1897 (Public Domain/Wikimedia Commons).

St. Columba and the Loch Ness Monster pg. 38: *Saint Columba converting the Picts* by William Hole (Public Domain/Wikimedia Commons); Loch Ness Monster (1660674010), image derived from Daniel Eskridge/shutterstock.com.

Memento Mori: The Church Faces Death part 2 pg. 47: Human Skulls wall panel (2208308613), image derived from Prasit Rithtem/ shutterstock.com.

St. Francis Kneeling in a Grotto pg. 50: *Saint Francis Kneeling in a Grotto, holding a Book and a Skull* by Nicolaas van der Horst (Public Domain/Wikimedia Commons).

Capuchin Crypt pg. 54: Capuchin Crypt (Public Domain/Wikimedia Commons); Roma cappella mortuaria nella chiesa dei Cappuccini (Public Domain/Wikimedia Commons).

Sedlec Ossuary pg. 62: Schwarzenberg coat-of-arms (90685135), image derived from Mikhail Markovskiy/shutterstock.com.

Capuchin Mummies pg. 66: In der Kapuzinergruft in Brünn (Public Domain/Wikimedia Commons).

Ars Moriendi: The Art of a Good Death pg. 71: Believer prays to God on knees (2226296191), image derived from AVA Bitter/shutterstock.com.

St. Cecilia Marble Statue pg. 76: Cornelis Galle, Graftombe van de H. Cecilia in de Santa Cecilia in Trastevere in Rome (Public Domain/ Wikimedia Commons).

The Museum of Purgatory pg. 142: *Fingerprints on an Old Prayer Book* by Emma Helstrom.

Poltergeist from The Wizard Clip pg. 146: *Poltergeist-Therese Selles* (Public Domain/Wikimedia Commons).

Cut-Up Cloth pg. 151: *Cut-Up Cloth with a Crescent Shape* by Emma Helstrom.

Fr. Amorth pg. 158: Don Gabriele Amorth by Angela Musolesi (Public Domain/Wikimedia Commons) image adjusted to line art, adjust facial expression of subject, and add in crucifix; Catholic cross (2358657851), image derived from Maisei Raman/shutterstock.com.

Exorcism pg. 168: *Exorcism* by Jean Delvin (Public Domain/Wikimedia Commons).

St. Michael the Archangel pg. 174: Saint Michael the archangel (2338367635), image derived from Immaculate/shutterstock.com.

St. Benedict of Nursia pg. 176: *St. Benedict in Ecstasy* by Claude Mellan (Public Domain/Wikimedia Commons).

The St. Benedict Medal pg. 178: The Saint Benedict Medal (2408869007), image derived from Allexxe/shutterstock.com.

Unusual Miracles part 4 pg. 181: Hand drawn holy tabgha fresh (2040257183), image derived from ArtMari/shutterstock.com.

Mother Cabrini pg. 185: *Mother Cabrini* by L. Caracciolo (Public Domain/Wikimedia Commons).

Miracle Water Fountain pg. 186: *Miracle of Mother Cabrini* by Emma Helstrom.

St. Francis of Assisi Receives the Stigmata pg. 188: *H. Franciscus van Assisi ontvangt de stigmata* by Hieronymus Wierix (Public Domain/Wikimedia Commons).

About the Author

ROM HIS HOME in the Rockies, Michael Lichens is an author, editor, and researcher with a passion for the overlooked aspects of Christian history. He is the former editor of *Catholic Exchange* and *St. Austin Review* and has appeared in numerous Catholic and mainstream publications. He is also a frequent guest on radio and television shows, on which he shares strange and delightful things about faith and history. With an MA from the University of Chicago Divinity School and a BA in Philosophy, Michael especially loves reading anything about St. Augustine and G. K. Chesterton. When he's not busy writing about bone churches and local history, he can be found editing books for authors or leading tours of old buildings in the American West or in Rome. Follow his writing and other adventures at mlichens.com.

Sophia Institute

Sophia Institute is a nonprofit institution that seeks to nurture the spiritual, moral, and cultural life of souls and to spread the gospel of Christ in conformity with the authentic teachings of the Roman Catholic Church.

Sophia Institute Press fulfills this mission by offering translations, reprints, and new publications that afford readers a rich source of the enduring wisdom of mankind.

Sophia Institute also operates the popular online resource CatholicExchange.com. *Catholic Exchange* provides world news from a Catholic perspective as well as daily devotionals and articles that will help readers to grow in holiness and live a life consistent with the teachings of the Church.

In 2013, Sophia Institute launched Sophia Institute for Teachers to renew and rebuild Catholic culture through service to Catholic education. With the goal of nurturing the spiritual, moral, and cultural life of souls, and an abiding respect for the role and work of teachers, we strive to provide materials and programs that are at once enlightening to the mind and ennobling to the heart; faithful and complete, as well as useful and practical.

Sophia Institute gratefully recognizes the Solidarity Association for preserving and encouraging the growth of our apostolate over the course of many years. Without their generous and timely support, this book would not be in your hands.

www.SophiaInstitute.com
www.CatholicExchange.com
www.SophiaTeachers.org

Sophia Institute Press is a registered trademark of Sophia Institute.
Sophia Institute is a tax-exempt institution as defined by the
Internal Revenue Code, Section 501(c)(3). Tax ID 22-2548708.